100 THINGS TO DO IN SHEBOYGAN BEFORE YOU DIE

Sheboygan Selfie Station at Deland Park

100 THINGS TO DO IN SHEBOYGAN BEFORE YOU DIE

LORI HELKE

Reedy Press
PO Box 5131
St. Louis, MO 63139, USA
reedypress.com

Library of Congress Control Number: 2024949289

ISBN: 9781681065724

Design by Jill Halpin

Cover photo courtesy of Lori Helke

Unless otherwise noted, all photos are courtesy of the author or believed to be in the public domain.

Printed in the United States of America
25 26 27 28 29   5 4 3 2 1

DEDICATION

To Rick, my fiercest supporter, and Megan,
who has inherited my love of travel.

River Boardwalk

CONTENTS

Music and Entertainment

Sports and Recreation

Culture and History

Shopping and Fashion

Sheboygan Lighthouse

Sheboygan Visual Arts

ACKNOWLEDGMENTS

I would not have been able to write this book without the constant support of Visit Sheboygan, particularly my friend and Visit Sheboygan's public relations manager Shelly Harms and president/CEO Amy Wilson. I was able to give my firsthand expertise on a vast majority of the things I mention in this book because of them. The fact that I also serve on the Visit Sheboygan board of directors has given me an inside scoop on all the great things in Sheboygan. I am eternally grateful to be a part of this organization that is dedicated to spotlighting Sheboygan as a premier tourist destination.

I have to thank Midwest Travel Network and its founders, Sara Broers and Lisa Trudell, for their encouragement and support. It's because of them that we have a wonderful group of writers and destination partners who live and breathe promoting Midwest travel. I'm proud to be among the many authors in the network.

Thank you to Reedy Press for this opportunity and for creating such incredible travel guides.

Last, I want to thank my family and friends for their support. It's because of all of you that I can confidently pursue this dream I am living.

PREFACE

I can attest to taking for granted all the things there are to see and do in your own backyard. I have done this for years. I was born in Sheboygan and have lived my whole life just a little over 20 miles away. Yet, I never realized just what a fantastic city Sheboygan is. That was until I pursued a second career as a travel blogger. I began to look at Sheboygan through fresh eyes. I became a tourist in this city. I found out what a wonderful foodie destination Sheboygan is. I discovered all the incredible gems there are here. Access to world-class art in the John Michael Kohler Arts Center and Art Preserve and public art popping up constantly. A wonderful theater venue. Lots of shopping and history.

What has captured my heart is the thing that has always been there. Sheboygan sits on the shores of Lake Michigan. If you didn't know any better, you'd swear you were looking out onto the ocean while standing on its shoreline. The beaches are soft sand, wide, and long. During winter, freshwater surfing enthusiasts ride the lake's angry waves, hence Sheboygan being named Malibu of the Midwest. In summer, it's a beach lover's paradise. Lake Michigan and the Sheboygan River, which runs into the lake, are focal points for much of the outdoor activity in Sheboygan.

Because of all that Sheboygan has to offer not only visitors but also those who live here, I want to share it with the world.

In this book, you'll find outstanding things to do, places to eat, and things to see in Sheboygan along with a few picks within 30 minutes of the city. When I shared with friends and family that I was writing this book, I consistently heard the question, "There's really 100 things to do in Sheboygan?"

Why, yes, there certainly are, and so much more.

Il Ritrovo Pizza

FOOD AND DRINK

1

SAVOR THE AUTHENTIC ITALIAN FLAVORS
AT LINO RISTORANTE ITALIANO

The first thing you need to know is that Sheboygan is a foodie city. While many regions and cuisines are represented, Italian food has made its mark. With my first of the 100 things to do in Sheboygan, we take a trip to the Mediterranean and have a dinner experience at Lino Ristorante Italiano. Lino's creates dishes with flavors that dance in your mouth using fresh ingredients and imported Italian components. The atmosphere is elegant, and the staff is knowledgeable and friendly. There is an extensive wine list to choose from, or enjoy a uniquely crafted cocktail. May I suggest starting with calamaretti fritti, calamari lightly floured and fried to perfection, then farfalle con portobello e gorgonzola if it's on the menu and you love mushrooms. Any of Lino's handmade pasta dishes are supreme, and please don't skip dessert.

422 S Pier Dr., 920-457-5200
linoitalia.com

TIP

I highly recommend ordering the tiramisu for dessert.

2

ENJOY THE BEST BARBECUE IN TOWN
AT PARKER JOHN'S BBQ & PIZZA

"I like pig butts and I cannot lie."

The servers often wear T-shirts that bear the above saying.

I may be biased, but I have a (smoky) sweet spot for this favorite. Parker John's began as a pizza place in my hometown of Kiel in 2008. After acquiring a smoker, it soon became the place for barbecue. Parker John's BBQ & Pizza quickly spread to multiple locations, including Sheboygan. The Sheboygan location on the river makes it an excellent spot for outdoor dining on the deck in summer. Locals think it's the best barbecue this side of Kansas City, and visitors agree. The sides and sauces are all made in-house. May I suggest combining two favorites, mac and cheese and pulled pork. Choose which takes center stage—the pulled pork with the Pig Mac or the mac and cheese with the Smokehouse Mac Bake. If you love Bloody Marys, Parker John's has the best, from just your classic Bloody Mary served with the usual fixings and a sausage stick to the Pitmaster Bloody. The Pitmaster Bloody is a 25-ounce Bloody Mary with a pork slider, chicken wings, a half rack of ribs, and sausage.

705 Riverfront Dr., 920-453-0299
parkerjohns.com/sheboygan

3

INDULGE IN AUTHENTIC MEXICAN FOOD
AT COCINA MI FAMILIA

If you are craving authentic, fresh, made-to-order Mexican food, the newly renovated Cocina Mi Familia has you covered. Sheboygan has a growing diverse food scene, and Mexican is well represented here. The exterior of this small restaurant may be unassuming, but the food is anything but. This family-owned restaurant takes traditional dishes from the Mexican state of Veracruz and blends those flavors to create an inspiring menu. Start with house-made chips and guacamole. Then have quesabirria tacos and wash them down with the restaurant's famous horchata. The remodeled interior is family friendly, clean, and well decorated, not over the top. Patrons come from all over and rave about Cocina Mi Familia as being their favorite Mexican restaurant in Sheboygan. Cocina Mi Familia serves breakfast all day. The prices are right, and the meals are served in generous portions. Don't forget dessert.

1423 Union Ave., 920-287-7039

TIP

If you love a great mole sauce, try the enchiladas de mole con pollo.

OTHER MEXICAN FOOD OPTIONS

La Conquistadora

1218 Indiana Ave., 920-458-5070

Las Brisa's

1129 S 8th St., 920-803-0440

Pacifico Bar & Grill

820 Indiana Ave., 920-395-2084
pacificobarandgrill.com

4

GET A TASTE OF TRUE NEAPOLITAN PIZZA
AT IL RITROVO

My mouth is watering just thinking about this pizza!

Opened in 2000 and the fifth certified Vera Pizza Napoletana restaurant in the US, Il Ritrovo will transport you to the Campania region of Italy. People come from all over to have this unique pizza. The crust is made from slow-fermented dough, and the tomatoes come from San Marzano.

No visit to Sheboygan is complete without having pizza at Il Ritrovo. The warm, chewy crust; the tang of those sun-kissed tomatoes; melted, flavorful, fresh mozzarella; and a delicious variety of toppings will knock your Italian loafers off. The pizza is worth the stop, and I love the lively atmosphere. The best way to enjoy a meal here is to each order different pizzas and then taste test. This is what I do when I am here with friends. I don't mind heating leftover pizza in the air fryer the next day.

My favorite is Boscaiola—chef's kiss.

515 S 8th St., 920-803-7516
ilritrovopizza.com

TIP

If you'd rather enjoy Il Ritrovo pizza at home, pick up a frozen one from Stefano's Slo Food Market around the corner.

OTHER PLACES TO GET AMAZING PIZZA

Uptown Slice

1116 Michigan Ave., 920-287-7098
uptownslice.com

Faye's Pizza

1821 Calumet Dr., 920-458-4171
fayespizza.com

Peabody's Pizza Co.

1123 N 8th St., 920-452-2702
peabodyspizza.com

5

COOL OFF
AT BLAST SOFT SERVE

On a hot summer day, there's nothing better than getting a frozen treat from this popular walk-up soft-serve stand. Prepare for a wait since the line can get long, but it goes fast. It's the only place in town that serves Dole Whip (traditional and raspberry), a favorite of mine since visiting the Dole Plantation in Oahu. Blast Soft Serve is located near the marina, Deland Park, and downtown, and it's the perfect stop after an afternoon enjoying the beach and the water. Cones, cups, sundaes, slushies, and flurries are served with a smile. If I am not having Dole Whip, I am indulging in a cookie dough flurry. The kids love the triple rainbow cone, and bring your pup along to enjoy a pup cup. New for 2024, Chester's Drive-In has added a food truck on the property.

Blast is open every day at 11 a.m. from April to the end of October. Watch the Facebook page for closing and opening dates.

406 Pennsylvania Ave., 920-453-0011
facebook.com/BlastSoftServe

TIP

Blast Soft Serve also serves lactose-free soft serve.

6

ENJOY FARM-TO-TABLE FOOD
AT FIELD TO FORK

Field to Fork is the third in the family of Sheboygan restaurants owned by Stefano Viglietti and his wife, Whitney. This book also lists his other two, Il Ritrovo and Trattoria Stefano. Field to Fork is a favorite breakfast and lunch spot focusing on fresh local ingredients and creative healthy options. A list of local Wisconsin suppliers is written on the huge chalkboard behind the counter.

Walking in, you immediately notice the lively buzz of conversation, colorful atmosphere, and energetic staff. It's always busy, so prepare for a wait. The restaurant offers inside counter or table seating, or outside seating.

Field to Fork offers an extensive beverage menu with cocktails, raw juices, smoothies, coffee, and tea. If it's lunch, I'll choose an Aperol Spritz. For breakfast, a lavender latte. Try the Quiché & Two (quiche of the day with salad and soup) or the beet salad for breakfast and lunch.

511 S 8th St., 920-694-0322
fieldtoforkcafe.com

7

HAVE DINNER
AT THE AWARD-WINNING BLACK PIG

The atmosphere inside Black Pig is just as classy and inviting as the food. The exposed cream city brick, dark wood, and beautiful stained glass window serve as an excellent backdrop to the menu. Locally sourced ingredients are the basis of creative twists on comfort foods. Start with white truffle and black pepper bacon fries, add porcini mushroom and potato gnocchi, or try the Big Pig Burger; no matter what you have, your taste buds will dance in delight.

The menu offers gluten-free and vegetarian options. It also includes an extensive cocktail, whiskey, and wine list. In fact, Black Pig was recently awarded the 2024 Best of Award of Excellence by *Wine Spectator*. Winners in this category must have a diverse selection of at least 90 quality wines that pair well with the menu and satisfy sophisticated wine lovers.

821 N 8th St., 920-457-6565
eatblackpig.com

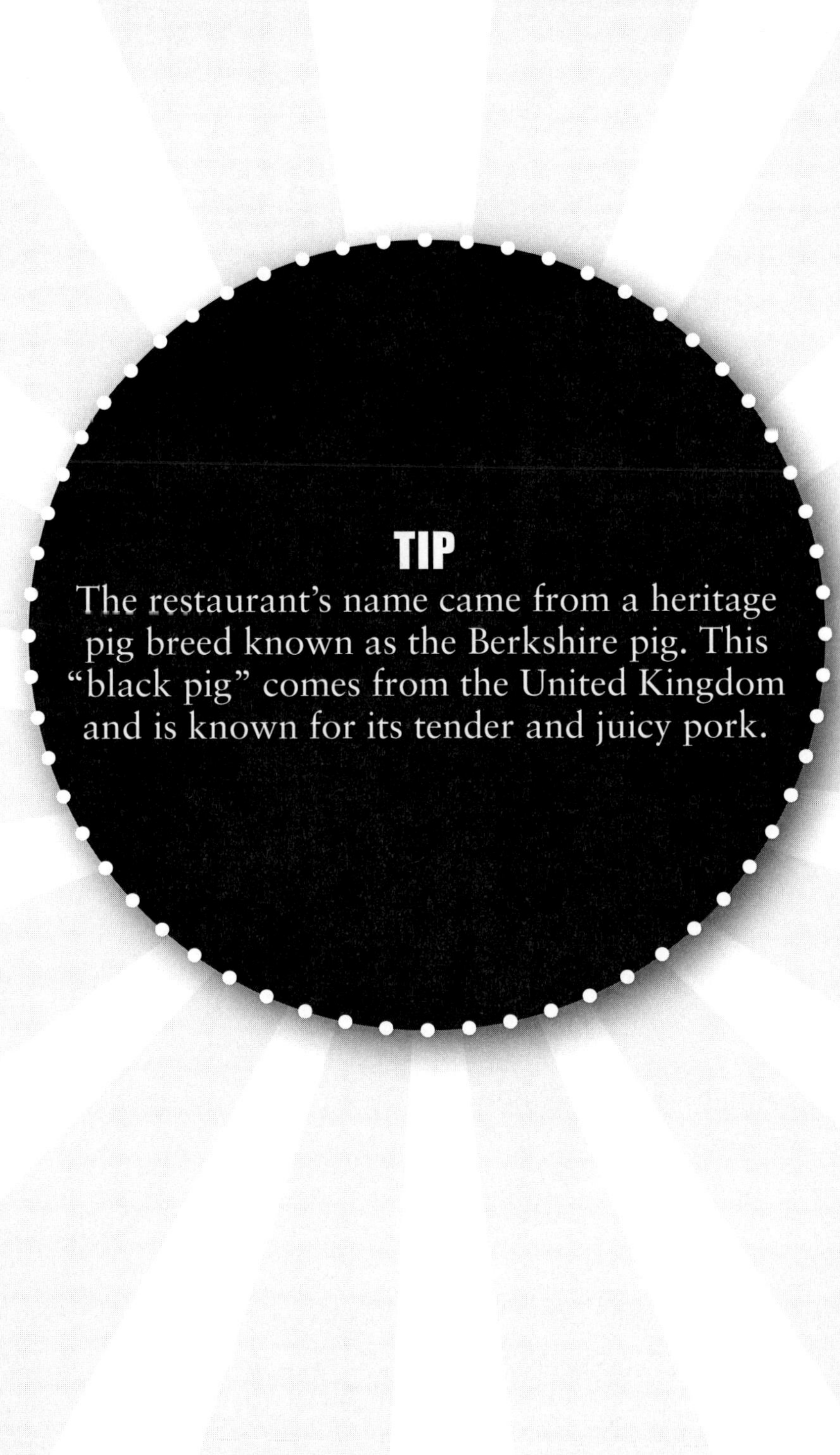

TIP

The restaurant's name came from a heritage pig breed known as the Berkshire pig. This "black pig" comes from the United Kingdom and is known for its tender and juicy pork.

8

CELEBRATE A SPECIAL OCCASION

AT TRATTORIA STEFANO

Experiencing a special dinner at Trattoria Stefano will carry you away to Italy. Imagine white tablecloths, linen napkins, and fine wine in an intimate setting. It's well-known that patrons from as far as Chicago will make a special trip to Sheboygan to dine at the first of Stefano Viglietti's restaurants. Taste authentic Italian dishes made from fresh ingredients, local and from carefully selected partners in Italy. Fresh, house-made pasta, sauces made with San Marzano tomatoes, and house-made sausages will tantalize your waiting taste buds. Try the chicken stuffed with truffle butter served with roasted potatoes and zucchini.

This isn't fast food; this is a lengthy romantic dinner, or a special birthday celebration with friends. Fun fact: If you park in front of the restaurant at the right time, you may catch one of the formally dressed servers crossing the street, bringing back a basket with freshly made bread from Field to Fork across the road. It's a fun sight.

Reservations are recommended.

522 S 8th St., 920-452-8455
trattoriastefano.com

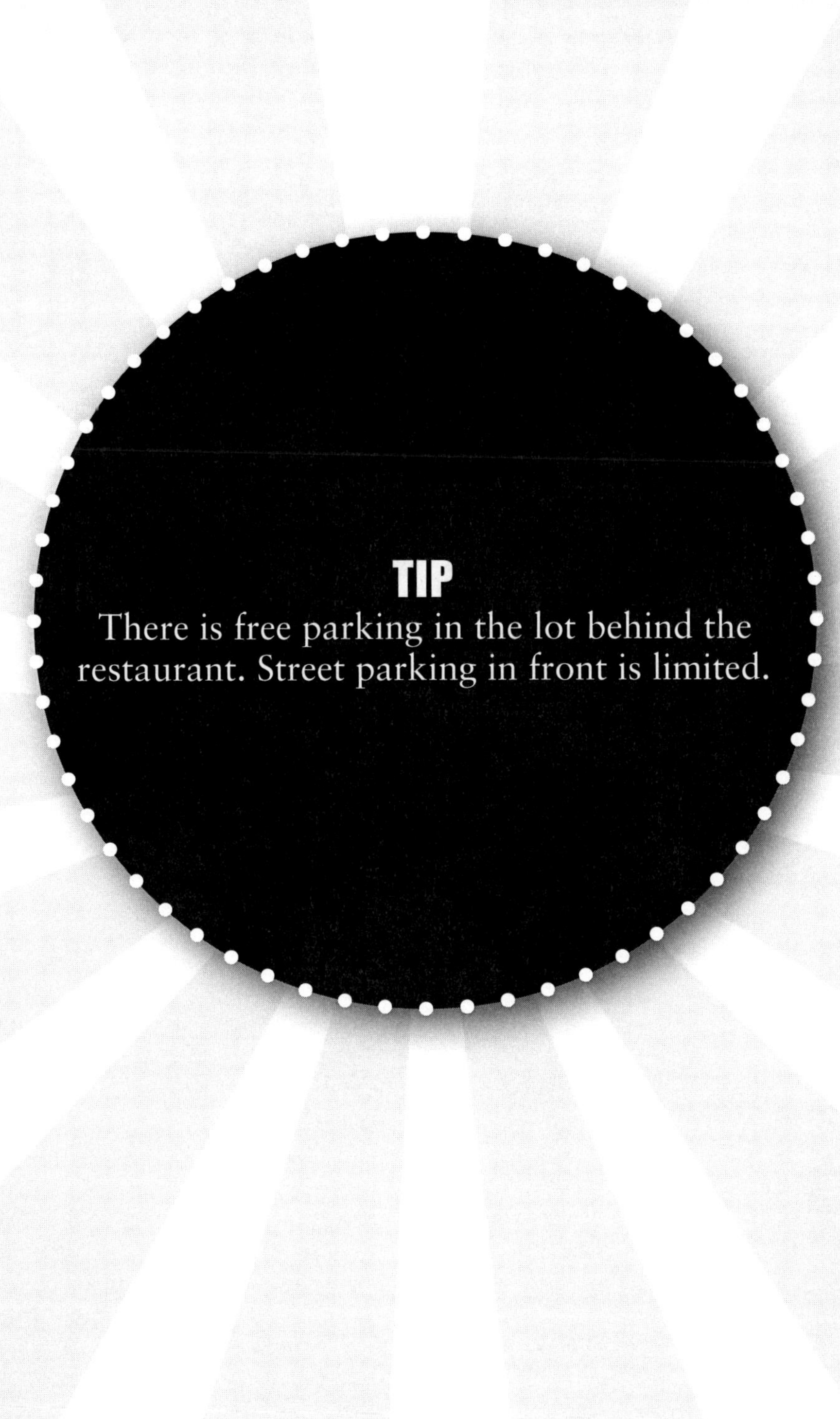

TIP

There is free parking in the lot behind the restaurant. Street parking in front is limited.

9

TAKE THE
FRANKIE'S PUB AND GRILL CHALLENGE

This unassuming, classic Wisconsin tavern on Indiana Avenue has a famous challenge that many try to conquer. Finish its 5.5-pound quadruple bacon cheeseburger in 45 minutes and you'll earn yourself a prized T-shirt proclaiming your accomplishment to the world. That's a whole lot of delicious burger. Believe me, it's not a challenge for the faint of heart.

Of course, if you aren't in the competitive spirit, you and some friends could split one for a great photo op.

Frankie's also has other classic pub fare on the menu. They serve 12-ounce burgers "as big as your head" on a Sheboygan hard roll, and other sandwiches. The double steak sandwich is sensational and highly recommended. The standard fried cheese curds are a must. You'll get great food in a lively bar atmosphere.

Do you think you're up for the challenge?

2218 Indiana Ave., 920-459-7000
frankiespubgrill.com

10

CELEBRATE THE OLD-FASHIONED DINER

AT HARRY'S DINER

Elvis is in the building. Or rather, a life-size replica of Elvis greets you as you enter Harry's Diner. Red, white, and chrome decor takes you back to a time of rock and roll and the poodle skirt, which is the standard uniform of the servers at Harry's Diner.

The extensive breakfast and lunch menu features tried-and-true classics like omelets and burgers, alongside burritos and breakfast hash plates. I love a simple, nostalgic burger, fries, and thick chocolate malt. You can even enjoy a cocktail like the Raspberry Pineapple Fizz—raspberry vodka, pineapple juice, and champagne.

If you're an Elvis fan, Harry's serves the Elvis: two pancakes or French toast with peanut butter and bananas, topped with whipped cream and Cap'n Crunch cereal.

Harry's Diner is a local favorite open for breakfast and lunch every day except Monday. If you can't get to the original location on Calumet Avenue, there is another Harry's Diner with the same nostalgic vibe off the interstate.

2504 Calumet Dr., 920-458-5200

Harry's Diner at Interstate
4024 WI-42, 920-459-4530
harrysdiner.net

11

FIND YOUR FAVORITE BREW
AT 3 SHEEPS BREWING

Founder Grant Pauly has taken his hobby of brewing beer from a single brewing kit to one of the biggest breweries in Wisconsin. 3 Sheeps operates out of a 30,000-square-foot brewing facility and a massive 10,000-square-foot taproom and event space.

3 Sheeps doesn't just focus on one kind of beer; the brewmasters produce IPAs, lagers, stouts, ales, and every kind you can think of.

What sets this brewery apart from others is its commitment to the community. On Sundays, the taproom is open to local groups for fundraising at no cost to rent. Every month, they choose a local organization to receive $1 from every pint sold of 3 Sheeps Pils poured out of the tap. In turn, the community supports the brewery.

Take the brewery tour, order a flight to discover your favorite, or play bingo every Wednesday night. 3 Sheeps is a great place to hang out.

1837 North Ave., 920-395-3583
3sheepsbrewing.com

TIP

3 Sheeps is dog friendly, so bring along your four-legged friend.

12

HAVE A BRAT PLATE
AT SLY'S MIDTOWN SALOOON

Sheboygan is known as the "bratwurst capital of the world," and while there are several places to get that celebrated sausage, you can't go wrong with the famed brat plate at the local "dive bar" Sly's Midtown Salooon. The traditional Sheboygan-style brat is served as a double on a Sheboygan hard roll from City Bakery, *not* a hot dog or brat bun. Accompanying the brat is a healthy dollop of potato salad and a cup of baked beans with a special pat of butter.

Owners David and Janet Sly have been in business since 1993, but when the building was rebuilt after a fire in 2010, they added a small kitchen and began serving food. You'll find lots of locals enjoying a cool drink at this downtown bar.

Sly's is also known for its Hangover Burger, a burger topped with bacon, cheese, a hash brown patty, and a fried egg.

508 N 8th St., 920-783-6644
slysbarandgrill.com

13

SHOP AT MIESFELD'S
TRIANGLE MARKET

Speaking of the famous brats, you can find them at Miesfeld's in more than 25 varieties such as Cajun and pineapple teriyaki. Miesfeld's Triangle Market is the place to buy all your meat for grilling. This Sheboygan County favorite, which has been around since 1941, also has a large selection of wine, other beverages, and cured meats, and it is a great place to get your venison processed during deer-hunting season. Its easy-access location just off of I-43 makes it a great stop for people traveling north to Green Bay and beyond and south to Milwaukee.

Miesfeld's has a huge selection of items. I love their pot pies for when I'm in a pinch and don't know what to serve for dinner, and I love to stop here and stock up before I go camping. The old-style meat counter is always busy with people waiting in line to get their fresh cuts of meat. On any given Saturday, the outside shack hosts brat frys for local groups.

4811 Venture Dr., 920-565-6328
miesfelds.com

14

TRY A FUN DOUGHNUT
AT SUNDAY DOUGH

We're not talking about your plain old glazed doughnut here. This is artistry at work. These doughnuts will put a smile on your face. The creative flavors are as pretty to look at as they are yummy to taste. There are always-present varieties like maple French toast, s'mores, and strawberry shortcake, along with ever-changing flavors of the month. You can order a flight and share it with friends. I can't resist ordering enough doughnuts just to walk out with the pretty pink box. I have to hold myself back from purchasing all the cute Sunday Dough merchandise available.

What I truly love is that this local business is just one of many woman-owned businesses in Sheboygan, and who doesn't like to support a women-owned business? Owner Laura Andrews hit the spot with this unique doughnut shop.

1402 S 8th St.
sundaydough.com

TIP

The doughnuts sell out fast. I would suggest going to the website starting at 5 p.m. on Tuesday and placing an order for pickup during store hours Friday through Sunday.

15

GET THOSE FAMOUS HARD ROLLS

AT CITY BAKERY

If you're going to grill out, there is no better bun than the Sheboygan hard roll. City Bakery is arguably the best in Sheboygan, depending on who you talk to. The locals are fiercely loyal to their favorite bakery. City Bakery offers much more than the hard roll. They have some of the best doughnuts, cakes, and bread in Sheboygan. I'm a huge fan of the peanut squares, elephant ears, and éclairs. On Wednesdays, you can purchase authentic Fleischbrok, a bread roll containing cabbage and meat.

City Bakery has been in operation since 1939. It's nearly impossible to miss the giant mural on the side of the brick building going west on Michigan Avenue. Luckily, they also sell their bakery goods wholesale, so those famous hard rolls are available in many stores around the area.

1102 Michigan Ave., 920-457-4493
sheboygancitybakery.com

TIP

Stop in early if you want those Sheboygan hard rolls.

OTHER SHEBOYGAN BAKERIES

Johnston's Bakery

1227 Superior Ave., 920-458-3342
johnstonsbakery.com

West Side Bakery

1422 Indiana Ave., 920-457-3313

16

EXPERIENCE A WISCONSIN SUPPER CLUB

AT MAJERLE'S BLACK RIVER GRILL

The supper club is a Wisconsin institution and part of the state's culture. In Sheboygan, you can experience it at Majerle's. The setting is perfect. There are trees surrounding the restaurant, giving it a northern Wisconsin feel. Inside, the large windows in the dining room take advantage of the view where you can often see deer outside. The bar is abuzz with people conversing about their weeks, relaxing, and waiting for an available table while enjoying a Wisconsin old-fashioned garnished with a cherry and an orange slice.

The menu includes the classics: tenderloin, Broasted chicken, pork chops, and seafood. The scallops are delicious and my supper club go-to. The dinners are served with a choice of two side dishes.

There's just something about that tradition of dinner in a cozy, dimly lit room, with generous portions, a relish tray, and a Brandy Alexander to finish off that makes you feel at home.

5033 Evergreen Dr., 920-803-5115
blackrivergrill.com

GET AN ICE CREAM
AT SOUTH PIER PARLOR

Do you scream for ice cream? It's a hot summer day and no walk along South Pier is complete without a snack stop at South Pier Parlor. I love the old-time atmosphere and huge variety (around 32) of hand-dipped ice cream flavors and sorbets, which change daily. South Pier Parlor serves high-quality Cedar Crest Ice Cream made in nearby Manitowoc. I'm partial to having my double scoop served in a homemade waffle cone, but you can choose a cup instead. You can get sundaes, old-fashioned ice cream sodas, and even fudge in a variety of flavors.

Inside, you'll see a spacious counter, booths, a black-and-white tile floor, and a tin ceiling. For the best view, take a table outside. It's a great spot to watch the boats and kayakers on the river. South Pier Parlor is open from early April until the end of October.

434 South Pier Dr., 920-395-2675
southpierparlor.com

SKIP THE COOKING
AT FOOD TRUCK MONDAYS

Where can you go for dinner on a Monday night in Sheboygan that will satisfy the whole family? Food Truck Mondays has become a popular summer weekly event. So much so that it expanded to two downtown sites in 2024, Vollrath Park and Kiwanis Park. There are often 24 businesses that participate, serving all varieties of food and beverages from barbeque to gyros and coffee to cheesecake.

The trucks come from all over and the atmosphere is festive. Having this on a Monday night when so many restaurants are typically closed is genius. This weekly event runs from 4 to 8 p.m., usually beginning in May and running through October, weather-dependent. There is a private Facebook group (Sheboygan Food Trucks) where you can find out what trucks are where each Monday, as well as general information about the local food trucks and other events they attend.

Vollrath Park
2001 N 3rd St.

Kiwanis Park
726 Kiwanis Park Dr.

GRAB A DOG TO GO
AT SPARKY'S

Sheboygan may be the "bratwurst capital of the world," but sometimes you need something different. I will revert to simplicity. This means that easy, inexpensive delight, the hot dog. So when a hot dog will do, nothing beats this famous Sheboygan stand. Sparky's has been at its location on Eighth Street for 25 years. Craving a Chicago dog? You can get that here along with a chili cheese dog and the kraut dog. According to the owners of Sparky's, these three are their bestsellers. Actually, you can choose from around 12 different varieties of hot dogs. Sparky's also has nachos, tacos in a bag, ice cream, and chips.

Father-son duo Steven and Kyle Hemsing operate the business, which began in 2007. Their all-beef dogs are made on a roller grill. They pride themselves in having customers who come back year after year. Those who visited as kids who now have families of their own stop in. It's a tradition to come to Sparky's in summer.

S 8th St. and Riverfront Dr.

TIP

If you're looking for a cheap eat in Sheboygan, you cannot go wrong with Sparky's. Their hot dogs start out at under $4.

20

GO TO RUPP'S DOWNTOWN

TO ENJOY THE BEST STEAKS IN TOWN

New York strip, prime rib, tenderloin—it's all sensational at Rupp's. Friends and visitors have told me that a steak at Rupp's is one of the tenderest and juiciest steaks they've ever had. This restaurant is famous with the locals, and on any weekend night, you will find the bar filled with people catching up on the week's events. This Sheboygan restaurant has been around since 1979 and is well-known for its great menu. The atmosphere is nostalgic and cozy. I love the wall-size Sheboygan history mural in the dining room.

Besides steaks, Rupp's serves excellent seafood and chicken. My pick when I dine here is the scallops. They are perfectly cooked, melt in your mouth, and are never rubbery. Rupp's also has one of the largest salad bars in the county. Finally, what's more nostalgic than ending a great dinner with a Grasshopper or Brandy Alexander?

925 N 8th St., 920-459-8155

TIP

Saturday is prime rib night. This is a must-do if you are a fan.

GET YOUR STACK
AT VENE'S PANCAKE HOUSE

If you're like me, you enjoy going out for breakfast. If you love pancakes, you will love Vene's Pancake House. Even though they also serve lunch, the extensive breakfast options are the highlight. Vene's has fantastic eggs Benedict, the best biscuits and gravy around, and great omelettes. Whatever you choose, you won't be disappointed. But let's talk about those pancakes. You'll find 11, yes 11, kinds of pancakes from plain ol' buttermilk to bacon pancakes. I think you should try the sausage pancakes (the sausage is inside the pancake) with whipped cream on the side to get a mix of sweet and savory. Or how about New York cheesecake pancakes? You get three huge cakes that will satisfy even the largest appetite. Trust me, the kids will be begging to come back again and again.

The building is in a residential neighborhood, so you may miss it. It's a small place, and you may have to wait. Or better yet, call ahead and take out. Vene's is open from 6 a.m. to 2 p.m. Check the Facebook page for the days the restaurant is open.

1632 Michigan Ave., 920-952-5720
facebook.com/venespancake

ENJOY TUESDAY NIGHTS IN SUMMER
ON 8TH STREET AT 8TH STREATERY

From June to August, on Tuesday nights from 5 to 9 p.m., Eighth Street closes to traffic, picnic tables take the place of vehicles, sounds of live music fill the air, and you'll find people enjoying takeout food from the nearby restaurants. It's 8th Steatery. Participation is easy. There are five restaurants to choose from. Some, you can go inside, specify you want your food for 8th Streatery, order, and carry out. The others request you call ahead to order. Participating restaurants include Local Press Eatery, Legend Larry's, Il Ritrovo, Trattoria Stefano, and Stefano's Slo Food Market. You'll find the details on the website. It's a festive community atmosphere that I love and a great way to enjoy the summer outdoors during the week.

8th St. and Pennsylvania Ave.
8thstreatery.com

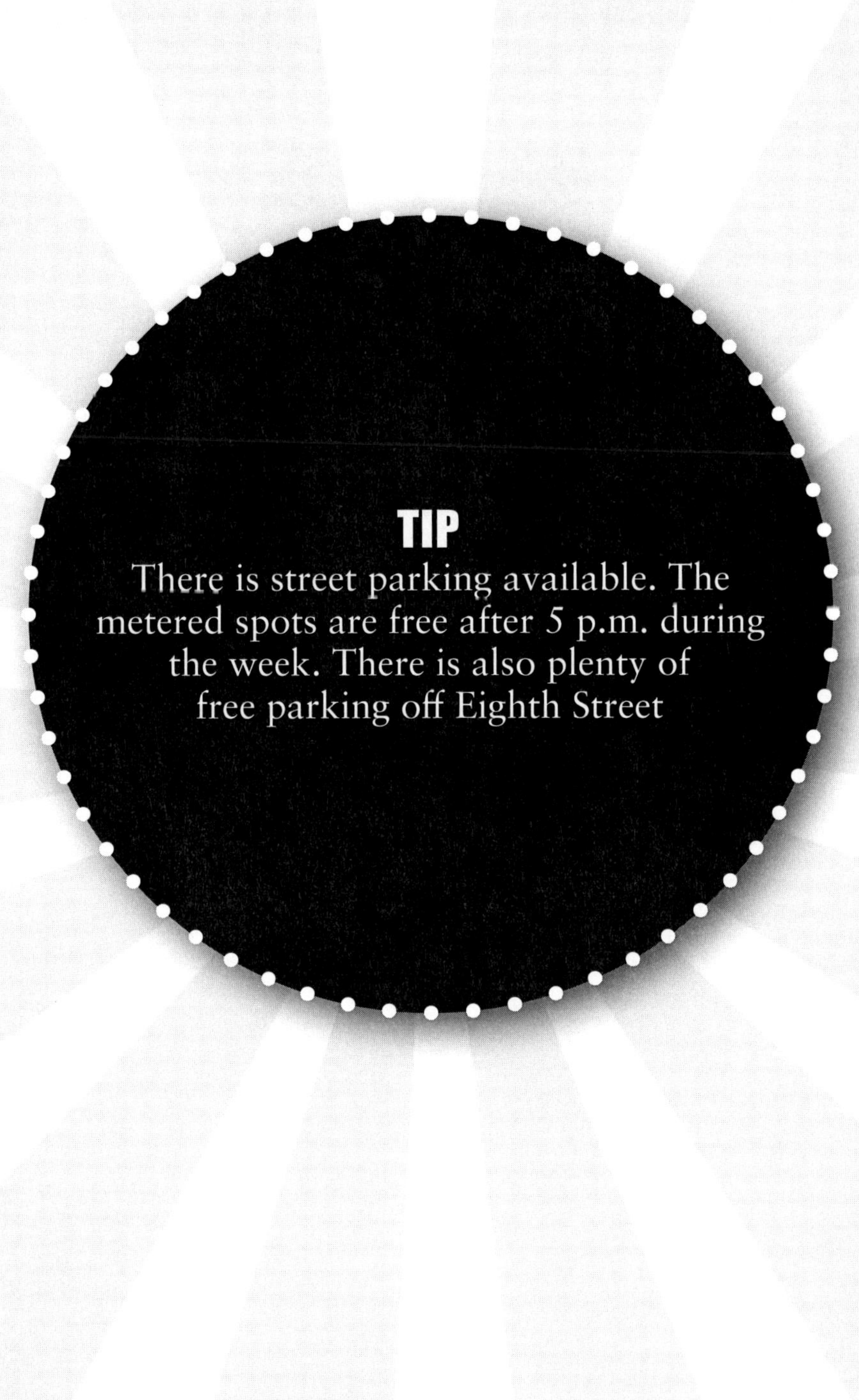
TIP
There is street parking available. The metered spots are free after 5 p.m. during the week. There is also plenty of free parking off Eighth Street

23

HANG OUT
AT PARADIGM COFFEE & MUSIC

There is so much to look at when you walk in the doors of Paradigm Coffee & Music. The vibe is industrial chic. A bicycle hangs from the ceiling. There's a wide assortment of items for sale. The bakery case is loaded with delectable goodies. It's a woman-owned, progressive, welcoming space for everyone to hang out, get some work done, read a book, or meet friends.

I love stopping in here, having a bagel sandwich and a frappé, and chilling out. You'll also find salads and soup of the day on the menu. There are a variety of vegan and gluten-free options too. Not only is there a selection of coffee drinks available, tea drinkers also have a large selection to choose from. There's plenty of seating. The portion of the street outside is closed off to traffic and tables are set up for visitors to savor the downtown experience.

Paradigm has an open mic night once a month and has live music too.

1202 N 8th St., 920-457-5277
paradigmvenue.com

OTHER PLACES FOR COFFEE

Weather Center Cafe

809 Riverfront Dr., 920-459-9283

eb flo

340 South Pier Dr., 920-917-9113
ebflo.com

EXPERIENCE A BIG-CITY MARKET
AT STEFANO'S SLO FOOD MARKET

Walking into Stefano's Slo Food Market is like stepping into a high-end neighborhood market in New York City. There are hot and cold food cases for takeout, a meat and seafood counter, yummy bakery and dessert items, and grocery items from around the world. A produce section is at the front of the market, and there's a wine selection to pair with any food.

I love it because you can find things you can't pick up everywhere, particularly a wide selection of food from Italy. I can even purchase the limoncello I brought back from Tuscany there. I like to stop in when I'm downtown for a quick lunch from the hot case. Usually, I will have arancini, those Italian rice balls, if they are in the case. The staff is knowledgeable and friendly.

731 Pennsylvania Ave., 920-287-7128
slofoodmarket.com

TIP

Slo Food Market is the fourth of Stefano Viglietti's establishments. All of them are on Eighth Street or around the same block.

25

CELEBRATE GERMAN TRADITION AT DER SHEBOYGAN BIERGARTEN

Sheboygan has deep German roots; after all, the brat reigns supreme. Another example of that German heritage is the traditional beer garden. Sheboygan has its own version in Kiwanis Park along the river, so dust off your traditional Bavarian lederhosen and dirndl and come on down for a pretzel and a liter of smooth pilsner.

They've got a wide selection of German beer served in half- or one-liter steins. Enjoy your brew with a giant pretzel or charcuterie, or bring your own picnic. (Monday night is food truck night.) Make it a family outing. The kids can enjoy a Sprecher root beer in a stein. Your leashed dog is welcome.

Before I go next time, I need to brush up on my German beer terms. What exactly is the difference between a pils, a helles, and a dunkle?

The biergarten is open from May through September.

511 Kiwanis Park Rd.
sheboyganbiergarten.com

TIP

Be sure to leave your cash at home. They only accept credit cards.

26

GO FOR A GIRLFRIENDS' NIGHT OUT

AT LUSHLOUNGE

When the typical bar scene just isn't what you want for a fun night out with the girls, LushLOUNGE is the best upscale alternative. The cocktails are delicious and fun, and the atmosphere is chic and comfortable. Beyond cocktails, you can get smoothies, lemonade, and coffee. Owners Christina and Colby Hephner enjoy having fun with their customers while making them feel right at home.

If you are hosting a baby shower, graduation, or birthday party, you can always have it at LushLOUNGE. Christina makes it all happen with ease.

Christina also owns LushICE, a luxury ice brand making ice cubes, spheres, and other shapes with edible flowers, fruit, words, and even premade drink ice. The ice business came first, and being a creative mixologist, she naturally moved into the cocktail space. I've never seen pretty ice until I saw Christina's ice. Her ice even ships to surrounding states.

1133 Michigan Ave., 920-287-1504

ATTEND AN ANNUAL FESTIVAL THAT CELEBRATES THE BRAT AT BRAT DAYS

Why wouldn't Sheboygan hold a weekend festival honoring its beloved bratwurst? After all, it is the "bratwurst capital of the world." This annual festival takes place at the beginning of August.

It is a tradition that started in 1953. The mayor at the time wrote a proclamation designating August 13 as Bratwurst Day. After 13 years of the annual event, it was shut down due to the behavior of certain eventgoers. It was brought back in 1978 in Kiwanis Park. The crowds steadily grew, famous national music acts were brought in, and in 1988, the Jaycees partnered with Johnsonville as the sponsor of the event. It remains the largest fundraiser for the Sheboygan Jaycees, and one of the largest events in Sheboygan.

There's a brat-eating contest, parade, cornhole tournament, beer, live music, and lots of brats to consume. If brats are not your thing, there are other options like hamburgers, corn on the cob, and grilled cheese sandwiches.

Kiwanis Park
brat-days.com

Sheboygan Marquee at Stefanie H. Weill Center

MUSIC AND ENTERTAINMENT

TAKE A DRIVE
THROUGH EVERGREEN PARK DURING THE HOLIDAYS

Evergreen Park, on the north side of the city, is lit up, inviting carloads of fans to drive through its annual holiday light show called Making Spirits Bright. Admission is free, but the donation of a nonperishable food item is suggested. Donated items go to the Sheboygan County Food Bank. A monetary donation is also appreciated to maintain the event.

You stay in the car during this 1.2-mile route that meanders through the park, which features various displays, including Whoville, a nativity scene, lighted tunnels, decorated trees, and a 20-foot "Mega Star." In 2023, more than 71,000 visitors came to see the display. Additionally, the Quarryview Center is open across the road for visitors to greet Santa and enjoy entertainment from local musicians after seeing the displays in the park.

Making Spirits Bright runs from the Friday after Thanksgiving until New Year's Eve.

Evergreen Park
makingspiritsbright.com

You can park your car across the street at Quarryview Center and take a trolley ride through the park on Friday and Saturday nights at 45-minute intervals beginning at 5:15 with the last ride departing at 8:15. The cost is $2 per rider.

LISTEN TO LIVE MUSIC AT THE BLIND HORSE RESTAURANT & WINERY

Friday and Saturday nights are the time to come to the Blind Horse Restaurant & Winery in nearby Kohler to see live music on the patio. Enjoy a glass of your favorite Blind Horse wine (or wine slushie), order food from the patio menu, sit back, and relax. The setting is fantastic, and there's no better way to unwind from a long week.

Want to know how Blind Horse got its name?

Way back in 1891 when the property was a farm owned by the Dreps family, the family had a favorite among the team of horses they owned. The name of this horse was Birdy. Birdy was a blind Percheron draft horse, hence, the restaurant and winery name when it opened in 2012.

If you cannot get there in summer, the Blind Horse is open all year. The restaurant has an upscale, creative menu featuring the signature filet mignon and the lobster ravioli. The winery and store are open all year too. To find out about events and specials, visit the Blind Horse Facebook page.

6018 Superior Ave., Kohler, 920-467-8599
blindhorsekohler.com

30

LISTEN TO LOCAL AND REGIONAL
JAZZ AND BLUES AT LIMELIGHT PUB

Limelight Pub stands as a typical Wisconsin bar on a corner lot within a residential neighborhood. At first glance, its facade might seem unremarkable, yet stepping inside unveils a scene that keeps patrons returning. The pub's menu offers delicious fare, but its true claim to fame is the live music that fills the air. Hosting a lineup of local and regional musicians from across the Midwest, Limelight features performances multiple times a week. Whether you're into cool jazz, gritty blues, or traditional folk, you'll find a vibrant mix of tunes that cater to diverse musical tastes.

The crowd at Limelight is just as varied as the music, with people of all ages gathering to enjoy the sounds. While the pub doesn't have its own parking lot, ample free on-street parking nearby makes it easy for visitors to swing by without hassle. Check the Facebook page for the most up-to-date lineup of music.

1702 S 17th St., 920-453-0233
limelightpub.com

BRING YOUR CHAIRS TO CITY GREEN THURSDAYS

FOR THE LEVITT AMP SHEBOYGAN MUSIC SERIES

The John Michael Kohler Arts Center hosts this free summer concert series as a way to bring the community together through the joy of music. It's a concert series that begins in June and is held on Thursday nights except for special events.

If you have live music, you need food too. Even though you can carry in your food and nonalcoholic beverages, there are food trucks available along with a beverage area. The kids (and adults) will enjoy the studio tent. Here you can engage in fun activities with an artist.

The concert series is a part of the Levitt Foundation initiative to bring free live music to underused outdoor spaces in a welcoming and diverse environment. This national foundation brings free music events to 45 cities across the country.

608 New York Ave., 920-458-6144
jmkac.org/engage/programs/levitt-amp-sheboygan-music-series

STAY CLASSY
WITH THE SHEBOYGAN SYMPHONY ORCHESTRA

If there is one thing about Sheboygan I love to spotlight, it is the wealth of cultural events and places in a city of this size. There are world-class museums, public art, and an abundance of live music to enjoy.

You can add a touch of sophistication to your visit to Sheboygan by attending a Sheboygan Symphony Orchestra concert during its season. Satisfy the classical music fan in you, or try something different. It is the longest continuously performing professional orchestra in Wisconsin. Founded in 1918, the group, along with the Sheboygan Symphony Chorus and the Sheboygan Symphony Youth Orchestra, performs inside the beautifully restored and opulent Stefanie H. Weill Center for the Performing Arts.

The symphony season runs from fall to spring with a collection of concerts that satisfy a vision of bringing community and music together.

830 N 8th St., 920-452-1985
sheboygansymphony.org

33

GET FARM-FRESH PRODUCE
AT SHEBOYGAN FARMERS MARKET

Wednesdays and Saturdays in Fountain Park come alive with the colors of summer. Those are the days the Sheboygan Farmers Market takes place. Although there are a few crafters, this market is primarily for purchasing fresh produce from the many vendors that tend gardens in the area. You can also find local meats, cheeses, bakery items, and a wonderful bounty of fresh flowers. You can come hungry because there are food and drink options too. This farmers market may be small compared to other cities, but it is mighty in variety and farm-fresh flavor.

The farmers market runs from 8 a.m. to 1 p.m. and kicks off in early June and runs till late October.

During winter, the farmers market moves indoors to First Congregational Church UCC on the first and third Saturdays of the month from 9 a.m. to noon.

8th St. and Erie Ave.
sheboygancountyinterfaith.org

TIP

Bring along a shopping or market bag. Many vendors have plastic bags, but I prefer the sturdiness of reusable bags, and they're environmentally friendly.

CATCH A SHOW
AT THE STEFANIE H. WEILL CENTER

The iconic theater marquee that lights up Eighth Street in downtown Sheboygan belongs to the Stefanie H. Weill Center for the Performing Arts. This venue, which is listed on the National Register of Historic Places, is a centerpiece of culture in a city that prides itself on the arts. The theater invites national and local acts in music, dance, theater, and comedy to its stage. Seeing a show in this opulent, restored venue is a wonderful experience whether you're seeing an AC/DC cover act or *The Nutcracker*.

The theater was originally opened in 1928 and was purchased by Warner Bros. in 1930. The company operated the theater until it was sold to Marcus Theatres Management Company in 1966. It closed in 1992.

Four years later an extensive five-year renovation process began, eventually restoring the theater to its 1928 charm with extensive updates to electrical, plumbing, and HVAC systems. A second grand opening took place in 2001. Today the theater is still going strong.

826 N 8th St., 920-208-3243
weillcenter.com

Sheboygan Harbor

SPORTS AND RECREATION

TAKE A SURFING LESSON
WITH EOS SURF SHOP

Learning to surf is almost a requirement for all visitors to Sheboygan. That is, if you are adventurous. You are in the Malibu of the Midwest after all. EOS Surf Shop offers two-hour lessons for individuals and groups. The price covers the gear needed (a wet suit since the water temp is cold.) The waves are unpredictable, so if there are none on your scheduled day, you can reschedule.

Did you know that Sheboygan's prime surf season runs from September through winter? That being said, if the winds are right, you will find surfers out all year-round.

If you'd rather just observe, watch from the beach at Deland Park and marvel at the dedication of those winter surfers. I always get a kick out of their ice-covered beards when they come out of the water. No thank you!

EOS also offers kiteboarding lessons and kayak and SUP rentals at its rental dock located at South Pier.

510 N 8th St., 920-208-7873
eossurf.com

SPEND A DAY
AT ROAD AMERICA

For those with a need for speed, a visit to Road America in Plymouth, just a short drive from Sheboygan, is a must. This is a legendary road course that twists and turns in a sprawling, parklike setting. It's one of the longest and most challenging in North America and has been thrilling fans and drivers alike since 1955. Road America's four-mile, 14-turn track is a true test of skill, making it a favorite among racing enthusiasts.

Race day isn't the only time you can visit Road America. There are several events and activities you can enjoy on non-race days. The famous Sunset Cruise is a way to check off a bucket list item. During summer, you can sign up to take a low-speed, three-lap spin around the track with your vehicle. On Monday and Thursday evenings from May to September, you can participate in 4 Miles of Fitness where you can walk, bike, or run the course. There is a fee for these events.

N7390 Hwy. 67, Plymouth, 800-365-7223
roadamerica.com

TIP

Everyone has a favorite corner or place to watch the race. Two of the best are Turn 5 and the Canada corner.

HOOK A CATCH OF THE DAY

ON A FISHING CHARTER

It's no secret that Lake Michigan is a highlight when visiting Sheboygan. Anglers come here from all over to go on a fishing charter on the big lake. It's an adrenaline rush to hook one of those huge salmon or trout that lurk in Lake Michigan's fresh waters. These charters all dock along the river downtown. Most charters offer half- and full-day excursions for up to six people, so take your friends or family on an adventure they won't forget.

Participation requires a Wisconsin fishing license and Great Lakes Salmon/Trout Stamp. I would suggest making sure you have sunglasses and a windproof jacket along with maybe a sweatshirt. Rain gear should also be brought along just in case even if it's sunny and 80 degrees. You will probably need to provide your own food, drinks, and snacks depending on how long you are out.

dnr.wisconsin.gov/topic/Fishing/outreach/FishingLicenses

FISHING CHARTERS

Dumper Dan's

676 South Pier Dr., 920-377-1147
dumperdan.com

Playin' Hooky Sportfishing

641 Riverfront Dr., 920-980-8557
playinhookyfishing.com

HI-TECH Sport Fishing Charters

690 South Pier Dr., 920-980-4031
sheboygancharterfishing.com

Slammin' Salmon Two

676 South Pier Dr., Parking Lot A, Slip #53
920-789-1400, slamminsalmontwo.com

Bucket List Fishing Charters

739 Riverfront Dr., Slip #78, 920-400-0083
sheboyganfishing.com

38

CATCH A SHEBOYGAN A'S BASEBALL GAME

Take me out to the ball game. A Sheboygan A's baseball game, that is. Going to a semipro baseball game isn't always about the sport. It's an inexpensive family-fun activity that not only appeals to sports fans but also to those (like me) who just enjoy the atmosphere of a live game. The A's are a part of the Wisconsin Baseball League and the Northeastern Wisconsin State League. The A's are made up of college-age players, and 41 of them have gone off to play professionally.

During the game, you can find a multitude of snacks such as cotton candy, pretzel bites, and nachos. Or how about a burger or brat? Wash it all down with a beer or soda. Between innings, the crowd enjoys fun activities and raffles to keep everyone entertained.

The season runs from May to August, and the home games are played at Wildwood Park on the corner of New Jersey Avenue and Wildwood Avenue.

2276 New Jersey Ave., 920-458-4377
sheboyganbaseball.org

KAYAK
THE SHEBOYGAN RIVER

The Sheboygan River meanders through downtown Sheboygan and is the perfect place to kayak. There are several public boat landings to launch from; the most popular spot is the accessible kayak launch in Kiwanis Park. You can follow the river in either direction. Eventually, you will find yourself at Lake Michigan if you go east. The route from Kiwanis Park to the lake is almost two miles.

If you don't have your own kayak, there are places for rentals. EOS Surf & Outdoor has a rental dock on South Pier Drive, or you can contact the shop and they will deliver a rental to your drop-in point.

If you would like to kayak and at the same time learn more about the area, take a Sheboygan River kayak tour with the Wandering Kayaker. This father-and-son duo offers a few different options depending on your interests.

The Wandering Kayaker
920-287-5774
thewanderingkayaker.com

HIT THE TRAIL
AT KOHLER-ANDRAE STATE PARK

One of the most beautiful state parks in Wisconsin is the nearly 1,000-acre Kohler-Andrae State Park, located along the sandy shores of Lake Michigan just south of downtown Sheboygan. It's a nature lovers' paradise that offers beautiful beaches, camping, and fantastic outdoor recreation. Probably the most used and unique feature is its two-mile Dunes Cordwalk Trail. I've hiked this in the early morning bright sunshine when a foggy mist hangs in the air. It's hilly but has incredible views. You may see sandhill cranes in this walk.

The park also has six other trails, each one a different experience. Throughout the year, there are candlelight hikes. There are lots of other opportunities for recreation in the park. A Wisconsin State Park sticker is required.

1020 Beach Park Ln., 920-451-4080
dnr.wisconsin.gov/topic/parks/kohlerandrae

CHECK OUT THESE OTHER TRAILS AROUND SHEBOYGAN

Old Plank Road Trail

The trailhead is located at Erie Avenue in Sheboygan and runs 21 miles to the Sheboygan County line along Highway 23. It then connects with the Fond du Lac County trails. The trail is paved and multiuse.

Taylor Drive Trail

This is a 3.3-mile multiuse trail connecting parks and shopping areas. There are several parking opportunities along the trail.

CTH PP Linear Parkway Trail

Covering 2.75 miles from Highland Avenue in Kohler to 17th Street in Sheboygan, this trail intersects with the Taylor Drive Trail.

You can find out more about these trails including maps on the Sheboygan County website under the Departments tab.

sheboygancounty.com

41

TAKE A HIKE
THROUGH MAYWOOD ENVIRONMENTAL PARK

Maywood Environmental Park is certainly one of those hidden gems in Sheboygan. There are eight different trails, each with a different ecosystem. Their distances range from 0.2 miles to 1.4 miles. There are 135 acres of lush forest, prairie, wetlands, and hills. Maywood is a city-owned park, free, and open all year. It's popular for snowshoeing in winter. This oasis is a fabulous place to watch the butterflies and hummingbirds as well as other wildlife.

There are year-round events for all ages, educational programs, and guided walks. One of the most popular events is Flapjack Day every March after the maple syrup has been tapped and made in the sugarhouse.

Most of the property was once a hobby farm that was donated to the city in 1973. The city eventually decided to turn it into a park, and Maywood was designated in 1983.

3615 Mueller Rd., 920-459-3906
gomaywood.org

WATCH THE KITEBOARDERS
ALONG KING PARK BEACH

Some surfers rely on the board and waves to glide on the water. Some attach a kite and speed along in a colorful spectacle to onlookers. Both make use of the unique Lake Michigan winds to enjoy their sport.

Head down to King Park or behind Blue Harbor when the winds blow and watch the kiteboarders. It's fun, fast, and (like I said) colorful against a wonderful blue sky. There's plenty of area on the sand to observe.

If you want to try kiteboarding, you can sign up for a lesson, or rent a board at EOS Surf.

If you don't want to get on the water, bring your land kite and fly away if you want to feel like part of the action. It adds to the colorful landscape; there is plenty of room to spread out on the beach or adjacent grassy area.

General King Park
1611 S 7th St.

TIP

There are a couple streets behind Blue Harbor that dead-end. You can park for free along them.

43

PLAY A ROUND OF GOLF
AT ONE OF SHEBOYGAN'S FAMOUS COURSES

Golfing is huge in Sheboygan County, made evident by the number of championship courses here. While most of us know Kohler for its quaint village and its bathroom and kitchen fixtures, Kohler is also famous for for its golf courses around the Sheboygan area. If playing at a world-famous, rugged, Irish-type championship course is on your bucket list, reserve a tee time at Whistling Straits. It's hosted the PGA Championship many times and the Ryder Cup and is just down the road along the lakeshore south of Sheboygan. Another famous challenging course is Blackwolf Run. This course has hosted past US Women's Open Golf Championships. The Bull at Pinehurst Farms in Sheboygan Falls is the only Jack Nicklaus–designed course in Wisconsin.

There are also several other courses in the area to conquer, if you'd like.

Whistling Straits
N8501 Lakeshore Rd., 800-618-5535
kohlerwisconsin.com/golf/whistling-straits

Blackwolf Run
1111 W Riverside Dr., Kohler, 800-618-5535
kohlerwisconsin.com/golf/blackwolf-run

The Bull at Pinehurst Farms Golf Course
One Long Dr., Sheboygan Falls, 920-467-1500
golfthebull.com

MORE BEAUTIFUL GOLF COURSES

Sheboygan Town & Country Club

W1943 County Rd. J, 920-467-2509
townandcountrygolf.com

Sunset Hills Golf Course & Driving Range

W3634 Sunset Rd., Sheboygan Falls, 920-467-0780
sunsethillsgolf.com

Riverdale Country Club

5008 S 12th St., 920-458-2561
riverdalecountryclub.com

Miller's Glen Golf Course

903 Madison Ave., 920-565-4536

Quit Qui Oc Golf Club

500 Quit Qui Oc Ln., Elkhart Lake, 920-876-2833
quitquiocgolf.com

CLIMB
PARNELL TOWER

Climbing Parnell Tower in Sheboygan County will give you a view of Kettle Moraine State Forest from 60 feet above the ground. It is the highest point in the Kettle Moraine. On a clear day, you have a 25-mile panoramic view of the surrounding forest and farmland. Parnell Tower is also on the Parnell Segment of Wisconsin's 1,200-mile Ice Age Trail. A portion of the trail overlaps with a relatively easy 3.5-mile loop trail. Camping is available at four campgrounds nearby in the Northern Unit of the Kettle Moraine State Forest. There are bathroom facilities, ample parking off the road, and a short walk to get to the tower.

You do need a Wisconsin State Parks sticker or day pass to access Parnell Tower.

W7876 County Hwy. U, Plymouth
dnr.wisconsin.gov/topic/parks/kmn/recreation

TIP

Climb the tower in the fall for a breathtaking view of the fall colors.

TRY YOUR HAND AT AXE THROWING
AT LONGHOUSE AXE BAR

It used to be that you went to your neighborhood bar, shot some darts, and played a few games of pool. I never imagined that the words *axe* and *bar* would mix, but the fun of axe throwing has made its way to Sheboygan with the one and only Longhouse Axe Bar. It's a fun sport and not as easy as it looks. Longhouse Axe Bar has 10 lanes that accommodate up to six people each. Pay for an hour or two of throwing. If you've never tried axe throwing, there is a technique to it.

If you don't want to participate, you still can be a spectator. The bar serves snacks and awesome craft cocktails.

Once you get the hang of it, you can drop in on Tuesdays for league night. I can say this is a fun group activity too.

1133 Indiana Ave., 920-453-0132
longhouseaxebar.com

46

EXPERIENCE WINTER FUN
AT BLUE HARBOR RESORT

No need to head to Wisconsin Dells when Blue Harbor Resort has an indoor water park. Called Breaker Bay, the water park is 54,000 square feet of fun. While it's primarily for resort guests, you can buy day passes on Sundays based on availability. There are water slides, a lazy river, a splash pad, a hot tub, and a surf simulator.

I love that the size is large enough for even older kids to have fun, while small enough to keep track of the younger ones.

If you need a break from the water, try mini golf, the arcade room, or the snack and drink bar.

While Breaker Bay isn't the mammoth size of some of Wisconsin Dells's indoor water parks, it is a fantastic way to spend a weekend getaway in winter.

725 Blue Harbor Dr., 866-701-2583
blueharborresort.com

TIP

Reserve a lakeside room with a patio, preferably not on the ground floor, to witness unforgettable sunrises.

TAKE A SEGWAY TOUR
OF SHEBOYGAN

Take a fun trip around Sheboygan, learn a bit about the history, and see some great sights along the way. A Segway tour with Glide N.E.W. is a great way to get an overview of Sheboygan, saving time and wear on your feet. You'll see the lighthouse, glide through the remains of a shipwreck, ride along the river, and head back into town. You can also customize your tour. Stop for lunch along the way at one of Sheboygan's many restaurants, or take plenty of pictures.

First, you'll get introduced to your mode of transportation and practice riding before you head off. I was intimidated the first time I got on a Segway but quickly got the hang of it. Your tour will last up to two hours including training. This is a fantastic family-friendly activity.

920-376-0256
glidenew.com

SWIM AT DELAND PARK
AND NORTH BEACH

Deland Park is home to the most popular swimming beach in Sheboygan. The long and wide stretch of sand known as North Beach and the gradually deepening water depth are great for little kids to wade at the shoreline. Sure, the water is cold most of the year, but in mid to late summer just about anyone can go in and cool off. It's a welcome relief from the summer heat and humidity of Wisconsin.

I grew up just 20 miles from the Lake Michigan shore and never took advantage of the gem I had right in front of me. Now I appreciate how lucky we are to have this fantastic swimming beach here.

There's often a game of volleyball taking place on the beach. Other amenities are playgrounds, restrooms, a bathhouse, a wheelchair beach-access mat, and access to walk out to the lighthouse.

901 Broughton Dr., 920-459-3440

STRAP ON THE ICE SKATES

FOR PUBLIC SKATING AT SHEBOYGAN LAKERS ICE CENTER

No matter your ice-skating ability, it's fun to get on the ice and practice your moves (or ungraceful falls). You can do that throughout the year (summers excluded) at the Sheboygan Lakers Ice Center. Most public skate times are on Tuesday, Wednesday, Thursday, and Saturday each week. Skate rentals are $3 and session prices start at $4. There are also skate lessons for hockey and figure skating. Book a birthday party either during public skate or a private party. The fee includes use of the party area and social hall. You can bring in your own food and drinks.

The ice center also is home to the Sheboygan Lakers hockey team and the Lakeshore Ice Sirens, the all-girl hockey team. Check out the calendar to find out the times of the public skate and other events.

1202 S Wildwood Ave., 920-458-3111
sheboyganlakershockey.com

EXPLORE SHEBOYGAN
ON SHEBIKIN'

Grab your friends for fun, celebrate a special occasion, explore Sheboygan, and get a workout all at the same time. Shebikin' is a peddle-powered tavern on wheels that has a captain in charge. Shebikin' can accommodate up to 15 people for the two-hour tour and needs a minimum of six peddlers to power it. The captain typically makes a few 15-minute bar stops along the route. You can bring along your own alcohol (beer and wine in non-glass containers only) and food on board. Participants must sign a waiver and there is a no-tolerance policy for inappropriate behavor. No need to worry about your fitness level. Five out of the 15 seats do not peddle.

If you want the same experience but on water, Sheboatin' does tours around Elkhart Lake in Sheboygan County.

920-676-3289
shebikin.com

51

GO CYCLING
AT EVERGREEN PARK

If you're looking for something other than the typical road cycling experience, the Sheboygan County Cycling group has been instrumental in maintaining and promoting its mountain biking trails. One of these trails is the Evergreen Park/Quarry Park trail. This six-mile intermediate trail has signage and winds through the park and across the road into the quarry property. The highest climb is 282 feet. This is a great place to learn mountain biking and is fun for the whole family.

The cycling group is intent on improving the cycling community in Sheboygan and is working with the International Mountain Bicycling Association to create a future master plan to expand this and other trails.

You can find trail maps and trail conditions on the Sheboygan County Cycling website.

Evergreen Park
sheboygancountycycling.org

HIKE OR SNOWSHOE
THE ICE AGE TRAIL

The Ice Age National Scenic Trail is 1,200 miles of segment trails with connecting road routes that meander along the glacial line in Wisconsin. There are three segments in the Kettle Moraine State Forest in Sheboygan County. While none run through the city of Sheboygan, those three segments run in the western portion of the county. The Parnell Segment is 12.9 miles, the Greenbush Segment is 8.7 miles, and the LaBudde Creek Segment near Elkhart Lake is two short segments connected by road. Many segments of the trail are not for the faint of heart as they go up and down hills and rocky terrain. The trail is open in winter for snowshoeing.

The trail is marked with yellow blazes, which you can see on poles, trees, and stakes along the trail. There are trailheads and free parking areas along the way. For trail updates, maps, and more, be sure to visit the website.

608-798-4453
iceagetrail.org

Every October, the Ice Age Trail Alliance celebrates the trails anniversary with the Mammoth Hike Challenge. Hike the anniversary number in miles and visit three trail communities within the month to earn a special patch. I've done this and it's fun, plus the fall colors make each segment hike magnificent.

53

GO CAMPING
AT BROUGHTON MARSH PARK

Broughton Marsh Park is one of the most popular parks in Sheboygan County. There are 50 campsites in two different sections of the park. Most sites have electric and some have water hookups. There are also tent sites available. The Sheboygan River runs through the 30-acre park, making it a great outdoor recreation destination. There are showers on-site, a dump site, and the Marsh Lodge restaurant, which has excellent food. You can also climb Wisconsin's largest wooden tower and get a bird's-eye view of the marsh. The park also has a foot golf and disc golf course, which is free to play, and a playground for the kids.

Campground reservations can be made by calling the number or through the Three Guys and a Grill website.

W7039 County Rd. S R, Elkhart Lake, 920-876-2535
threeguysandagrill.com

OTHER CAMPGROUNDS AROUND SHEBOYGAN

Plymouth Rock Campground

N7271 Lando St., Plymouth, 920-892-4252
thousandtrails.com

Sundance Farm Campground

W6224 Woodland Rd., Plymouth, 920-893-0384
sundancefarmcampground.com

Zig's Golf Haven

N8540 Lakeshore Rd., Haven, 920-980-9253
facebook.com/zigsgolfhaven

KOA Holiday Campgrounds

N5456 Division Rd., Glenbeulah, 800-562-0843
koa.com/campgrounds/kettle-moraine

TRY DISC GOLFING
ALONG LAKE MICHIGAN

Disc golfing is a great way to enjoy the outdoors any time of year. Disc golfers will love the challenge and picturesque setting of the 18-hole course at Vollrath Park. There are hills, trees, and the ever-present threat of losing a disc to Lake Michigan that make this course popular for beginners and more experienced enthusiasts.

You will also find the Shack, a disc golf shop in Vollrath Park that can supply you with all the gear needed. The Shack has new and used discs and some hard-to-find discs too. If you'd like to try the sport, stop in and ask about borrowing some discs to try on the course. Owners Dennis and Patty can help you out, supply a scorecard, and give you some pointers.

100 Park Ave., 920-208-0208
facebook.com/TheShackDG

TIP

I suggest using neon discs here since losing a disc is easy, and don't aim for the lake.

ANOTHER DISC GOLF COURSE IN SHEBOYGAN

Sheboygan Jaycees Quarryview Center

3401 Calumet Dr.

RENT A SUP AND PADDLE AROUND SHEBOYGAN QUARRY BEACH

Swimming at "the quarry" has been a thing for as long as I can remember. Today it's a family-fun, multiuse Sheboygan destination that attracts many locals and visitors.

Along with a huge inflatable aqua park, you can rent kayaks and paddleboards to take advantage of the calm water and great scenery on the quarry lake. You cannot bring your own with you. For safety reasons, everyone is required to wear a Coast Guard–certified life jacket. To enter the quarry, you must purchase a session pass for the beach or the aqua park. Reserving your session online saves you a bit of money compared to walking in. Sessions run for 90 minutes and are limited to 90 people. You can purchase extra sessions.

3401 Calumet Dr., 920-287-3303
sheboyganquarry.com

TIP

Don't forget to bring your Coast Guard–certified life jacket when you visit Quarry Beach.

56

WATCH THE SUNRISE
FROM SOUTH PIER

Catching a sunrise over Lake Michigan is one of those things that should be on everyone's bucket list. The colors flood the surf. To watch the sun with the sound of the waves rolling onto the shore is a feast for the senses and a wonderful way to start a new day.

There are several points in Sheboygan to see this, but the long and wide stretch of beach at South Pier is my favorite. It's usually very quiet, just a few early morning risers walking the trail behind Blue Harbor Resort. I swear you'll think you are in Cape Cod with the vast expanse of beach and the wild grasses growing up through the dunes.

There are street parking options all along South Pier Drive, or park behind Blue Harbor on the dead end on Illinois Avenue or Indiana Avenue.

End of South Pier Dr.

HIT THE MINI LINKS
AT HARBOR POINTE MINI GOLF

If you prefer the short links to the long challenging ones, stop at Harbor Pointe Mini Golf. Family fun awaits along the riverfront with a view of the lake at the only outdoor mini golf course in Sheboygan.

Harbor Pointe Mini Golf has 18 holes of fun. The course is clean and well maintained. Some of the holes are easy and some are more challenging, making this a great course for all ages. The kids love the nautical theme, lighthouse, and boat feature. There are snacks available and the prices are reasonable. Kids 4 and under are free with a paying adult. When you're finished, take the short walk to South Pier Parlor for some ice cream. There are also some fabulous eating options there.

Harbor Pointe Mini Golf is open from spring through fall. It's located across from Blue Harbor Resort.

322 South Pier Dr., 920-889-4190
hpminigolf.com

OTHER MINI GOLF PLACES AROUND SHEBOYGAN

Tom & Jerry's Mini Golf & Battling Cages

110 Suhrke Rd., Plymouth, 920-893-0045
tjminigolf.com

Sunset Hills Golf Course & Driving Range

W3634 Sunset Rd., Sheboygan Falls, 920-467-0780
sunsethillsgolf.com

TAKE A STROLL
ALONG THE RIVER BOARDWALK AND LAKEFRONT

The most scenic walk you can take in Sheboygan is along the lakefront starting at Vollrath Park or North Point Park, then go south to Pennsylvania Avenue, where you cross the street and continue on your way to the Riverfront Boardwalk. The boardwalk runs along the north side of the river past restaurants until Eighth Street. This is well over two miles. Here, you can cross the bridge and continue on to the South Pier Boardwalk, which has access to shops, restaurants, and recreational opportunities. The path is paved and accessible. There are many other points of interest along the way.

Parking spots are available for those who prefer a shorter walk. You also have easy walking access to Eighth Street, the main shopping street in Sheboygan. For me, this route is the heartbeat of Sheboygan. You can always take a detour and walk along the beach.

Lakefront and River

PRACTICE YOUR SWING
AT GOLF 365

When the harsh winter winds blow and you're feeling withdrawal from spending time on the course, Golf 365 is here for you. Actually, Golf 365 is open all year.

There are four simulator bays to get your game on. The cool thing is you can pick your course from 400 of the world's courses. Care to play St. Andrews in Scotland? Perhaps you'd like to golf at Whistling Straits without the high price? Done and done. You pay by the hour with weekdays being the cheapest time. Prices start at $30 for an hour.

No clubs of your own? That's not a problem; you can get clubs there. You can take lessons from a licensed pro, and after I highly recommend drink and pizza from Deo's Pizzeria and Pub (one of my favorite pizza places in Sheboygan County) at the full bar.

2729 Indiana Ave., 920-547-1655
golf365wi.com

Display at John Michael Kohler Art Preserve

CULTURE AND HISTORY

WALK THROUGH THE REMAINS OF A SHIPWRECK

The *Lottie Cooper* is on display across from the YMCA at Deland Park. This three-masted schooner sunk just off the Sheboygan coastline in 1894. It was built in Manitowoc in 1876 and capsized in gale-force winds. Five of the six crew members were rescued. The ship's remains were discovered in 1992 during the construction of the Sheboygan Marina and brought onshore for display. The *Lottie Cooper* is a reminder of the unforgiving force of the lake. The wooden remains are separated by a walkway for visitors to get up close. There are weathered signs detailing the schooner at the site.

Did you know that there are many more sunken ships in the Lake Michigan waters? In fact, there are 36 known shipwrecks inside what is now the Wisconsin Shipwreck Coast National Marine Sanctuary. The sanctuary covers the coastline from Port Washington, past Two Rivers.

Deland Park
Broughton Dr.

GO BACK IN TIME
AT THE HISTORIC WADE HOUSE

The Wade House served as a stagecoach inn between Fond du Lac and Sheboygan in the 1800s. This historical site pays tribute to horse-drawn travel with the displays inside the Wesley W. Jung Carriage Museum and Visitor Center, Herrling Sawmill, and Dockstader Blacksmith Shop.

My favorite is the Wade House Stagecoach Inn itself. This stately Greek Revival house is decorated from the period. Imagine tired and hungry travelers in all their finery, staying in beautiful guest rooms. See the kitchen that once served those guests, and also the bar where they could socialize.

The Wade House is more than just a peek into the past; it's an immersive experience that invites visitors of all ages to step into the rich tapestry of Wisconsin's pioneer days.

W7965 WI-23, Greenbush, 920-526-3271
wadehouse.wisconsinhistory.org

TAKE A SELF-GUIDED WALK

THROUGH AN EFFIGY BURIAL GROUND

This park is one of those little-known gems that even the locals overlook. Sheboygan Indian Mound Park is an ancient burial ground that's home to 18 burial mounds built by a nomadic Indigenous tribe that existed during AD 155–1000. In 1926, the Milwaukee Public Museum came in to dig up the site. In the 1950s, a group raised the funds to purchase the site and donated it to the city to be used as a park, and the museum oversaw the restoration.

Most mounds are in the shape of woodland animals, mostly deer. Some are conical in shape. Not only is this a quiet place for respect and reflection located within a wooded area, but it is also a fantastic stop for nature lovers. You can take a self-guided walk along the marked trail through the burial mounds and the wetland nature trail. The highlight of this park is the open mound burial display.

5000 S 9th St.
920-459-3340

LEARN ABOUT THE HISTORY OF THE KOHLER CO.

On the outside, the Kohler Design Center looks like just that, a place to go for help with designing the perfect bathroom or kitchen. Let me tell you, that is just the beginning. You do not need to be in the market for bath and kitchen fixtures to enter. The design center has three floors featuring the past, present, and future. There are complete room setups featuring Kohler's innovative designs that make you feel like you are walking through the pages of a magazine.

The lower level is dedicated to the company's rich history and the Kohler family with displays of past products and more.

It is also possible to take a factory tour through the design center. You can call ahead to find out about tour availability.

101 Upper Rd., Kohler, 920-457-3699
kohlerwisconsin.com/explore-more/
activities-and-events/kohler-design-center

SEE THE MODEL RAILROADS
AT SHEBOYGAN RAILROAD MUSEUM

Run by a passionate group of model-railroad enthusiasts, Sheboygan Railroad Museum is a great stop for railroad fans of all ages. There are eight model railroads on display of various scales and one specifically for the kids to operate themselves. Don't be afraid to ask questions. These conductors love to share their knowledge and stories about their love of all things in the model-railroad world. The museum is not always open, so check the website for times.

I enjoy stopping here just to look at the details of each display: a miniature city with models of old house trailers, a model of the Miller Brewing Company, and a bustling railroad station. The sound of the trains running on the track and the whistles remind me of my dad and his model-train setup years ago.

1001 N 10th St., 920-783-6248
sssmre.org/museum.htm

PAY YOUR RESPECTS
AT A VETERANS MEMORIAL

The Sheboygan County Veterans Memorial stands as a tribute to more than 4,000 veterans from Sheboygan County, their names etched on seven imposing granite pillars. Established in 1994, this powerful site continues to grow, with plans to expand its memorial wall. The tribute honors all branches of the US military, offering a solemn space for visitors to reflect on the sacrifices made. Benches throughout the site provide peaceful spots for quiet contemplation.

In addition to this memorial, the Lao, Hmong and American Veterans Memorial pays homage to those who fought and sacrificed during the US Secret War in Laos from 1961 to 1975. This memorial is not only a place to honor the fallen but also an educational space, with panels explaining the significance of the Secret War and the reasons Sheboygan is home to a large Hmong community today. Together, these memorials provide meaningful tributes to diverse stories of bravery and sacrifice.

Sheboygan County Veterans Memorial
3091 Wilgus Ave., 920-207-1196
scvmemorial.org

Lao, Hmong and American Veterans Memorial
Deland Park
laohmongusmemorial.com

LEARN ABOUT ARTIST-BUILT ENVIRONMENTS

AT JOHN MICHAEL KOHLER ART PRESERVE

Do you know what an artist-built environment is? I didn't until I visited this unique art museum. The John Michael Kohler Art Preserve's 37,000 square feet of gallery space encompass work from around 35 artist-created environments. These artists are often not formally trained, so they are unconventional in their creative processes. It is an interesting look into their minds. Most are driven to create like they need air to breathe.

The artists use unique materials found around them. Glass, wire, rope, concrete, and, yes, even chicken bones. Their art sometimes consumes their living spaces. Because of this, the work of each artist is presented at the art preserve grouped in a way to honor its original site. We have quite a few original artist-built environments in Wisconsin. Fred Smith's Wisconsin Concrete Park in northern Wisconsin is one.

Because of its theme, the 38-acre art preserve appeals to a wide range of people. You do not need to be an art connoisseur to appreciate it.

3636 Lower Falls Rd., 920-453-0346
jmkac.org/art-preserve/about-art-preserve

67

VISIT A REAL ARTIST ENVIRONMENT AT JAMES TELLEN WOODLAND SCULPTURE GARDEN

A true example of an artist environment resides in the Black River area on Sheboygan's south side. This property was once the summer cottage of James Tellen's family. It is now open to the public for visitors to observe the concrete works Tellen created between 1942 and his death in 1957.

The life-size figures, religious and mythical, dot the wooded path around the site. The figures have intricate, detailed expressions adding to the haunting feeling of the property. It is a peaceful spot to come to reflect where you can almost feel the spirits in the air. You will often see deer standing among the trees. The family cottage and "brat fryer" still stand on the property and are open to the public during special times. Another structure on the land is home to an artist-in-residence through the Kohler Foundation.

5634 Evergreen Dr., 920-458-6144
jmkac.org/artist/tellen-james

LEARN WHY SHEBOYGAN WAS ONCE KNOWN AS "CHAIR CITY"

AT THE SHEBOYGAN COUNTY MUSEUM

Between 1865 and 1980, there were 12 furniture manufacturers in Sheboygan. This is just one of the interesting facts from the displays at the Sheboygan County Museum. The museum shares the history of the county on a complex that is home to a cheese factory, an original log cabin, and a barn that were all located in the county and moved to the museum campus. The Taylor House is also open to tour and was built in 1853 for Judge David Taylor. It is an example of upper-class living during the period.

An extra special time to visit the museum is during the holidays when the original Prange's animated displays come out. You can also see "Bruce the Spruce" and the Santa Chair that was used in Prange's downtown. Many a child sat on Santa's lap while he was in that chair, including yours truly in 1967.

3110 Erie Ave., 920-458-1103
sheboyganmuseum.org

TIP

Go through the barn first, then make your way to the other buildings.

SEE THE TALLEST
SYMBOL OF FREEDOM

You cannot miss it while you are driving on Interstate 43: the Acuity Flag, that huge beacon of freedom waving proudly in the air. Did you know you can get up close to it? You can see it on the Acuity Insurance campus. At the foot of the flagpole, you'll see a veterans memorial featuring pavers with the names of Sheboygan County residents killed in active duty going back to the Civil War. There is a kiosk nearby with a map to help locate the names of veterans.

Standing right under it, the 400-foot flagpole looks like it could reach the sun. The flag itself is 70 by 120 feet and weighs 250 pounds. Each stripe on the flag is five feet tall and each star measures three feet across. It takes 500 gallons of paint to paint the flagpole.

2800 S Taylor Dr.
acuity.com/about/flagpole

TIP

Take Taylor Avenue to Acuity Insurance. There is a specific entrance to the flag, which is marked by a sign.

SUPPORT LOCAL ARTISTS
WITH A VISIT TO SHEBOYGAN VISUAL ARTISTS

Sheboygan Visual Artists is a co-op of artists, local and regional, that come together to promote their work, create events for the community to enjoy the visual arts, and empower each other through collaboration and professional development. They have a dedicated gallery space where the public can see and purchase the members' art. There are all forms of art from painting and sculpture to jewelry and mixed-media pieces. They also host several exhibitions, events, and workshops throughout the year.

The gallery is typically open every Saturday and is the only one I know of in Sheboygan. The space is open and welcoming, and the volunteers that are on hand are great at answering questions and sharing about their work and the organization. I enjoy going in to see the variety of art that is displayed and don't feel like I need to be an art expert to enjoy it.

1201 Erie Ave., 262-416-1278
sheboyganvisualartists.org

OTHER ART GALLERIES NEAR SHEBOYGAN

Gallery 110 North inside the Plymouth Arts Center

520 E Mill St., Plymouth, 920-892-8409
plymoutharts.org

ARTspace

725G Woodlake Rd., Kohler, 920-694-4534
kohlerwisconsin.com/explore-more/shopping-directory/artspace

Designs by Dieter

904 Monroe St., Sheboygan Falls, 920-980-7255
dietermetalart.com

Two Fish Gallery

244 E Rhine St., Elkhart Lake, 920-838-0626
twofishgallery.net

GO INSIDE THE BATHROOMS

AT JOHN MICHAEL KOHLER ARTS CENTER (EVEN IF YOU DON'T NEED TO GO)

Trust me, you've never seen bathrooms as exciting as those at John Michael Kohler Arts Center and Art Preserve.

The arts center started it all by commissioning six artists in the 1990s to transform the restrooms into works of art. Each one has a theme, and the colorful tiles are hand-painted and glazed to reflect the artist's imaginative vision for their space.

The children's studio washroom was designed in collaboration with the preschool students at JMKAC. It's my favorite. The children painted and glazed tiles with self-portraits, pets, and whatever came to mind. Can you imagine coming into this bathroom 30 years later to see the self-portrait tile you painted when you were 4 years old? How fun.

This idea spilled over into the restrooms at the art preserve too.

Don't be shy; you can view every restroom in the building, just be sure to knock before entering.

608 New York Ave., 920-458-6144
jmkac.org

EXPERIENCE THE WORLD OF AVIATION

AT THE AVIATION HERITAGE CENTER OF WISCONSIN

Take a ride out to the Sheboygan County Airport to see another often-overlooked place, the Aviation Heritage Center of Wisconsin. There are exhibits to honor Wisconsin flight history such as a commemoration to North Central Airlines, a Wisconsin-based national airline that flew between 1944 and 1979, when it acquired Southern Airways and was renamed Republic Airlines.

There are also other permanent exhibits, a Wright Brothers flight simulator, and annual events, including movie night on the second Friday of each month when aviation-themed films are shown.

The Sheboygan County Airport is one of the busiest private airports in the state, in part due to the nearby golf courses and the Kohler Co.

There is no admission fee, and the Aviation Heritage Center of Wisconsin is open all year, Wednesday through Sunday, and there is plenty of parking available.

N6191 Resource Dr., Sheboygan Falls, 920-467-2043
ahcw.org

SNAP A PHOTO
OF THE SHEBOYGAN LIGHTHOUSE

There's something about a lighthouse that makes a great photo. The big red lighthouse at the end of the pier in Deland Park is one you can walk right up to. In my opinion, the best photo op is right before the last stretch of the pier on a beautiful sunny day with blue skies as the backdrop.

You can also get a great shot at the end of South Pier with a professional camera. Extra points for a spectacular sunrise or stormy photo.

This pierhead light was built in 1915. The lantern room has been removed, but the tower is still an active navigational aid. There are weather monitoring devices and a foghorn in it. The lighthouse is not open to the public, but you can climb the steps up to it.

This makes for a nice walk when the weather is decent, and halfway to it is one of the best vantage points to watch the surfers too.

Deland Park
Broughton Dr., 920-459-3440

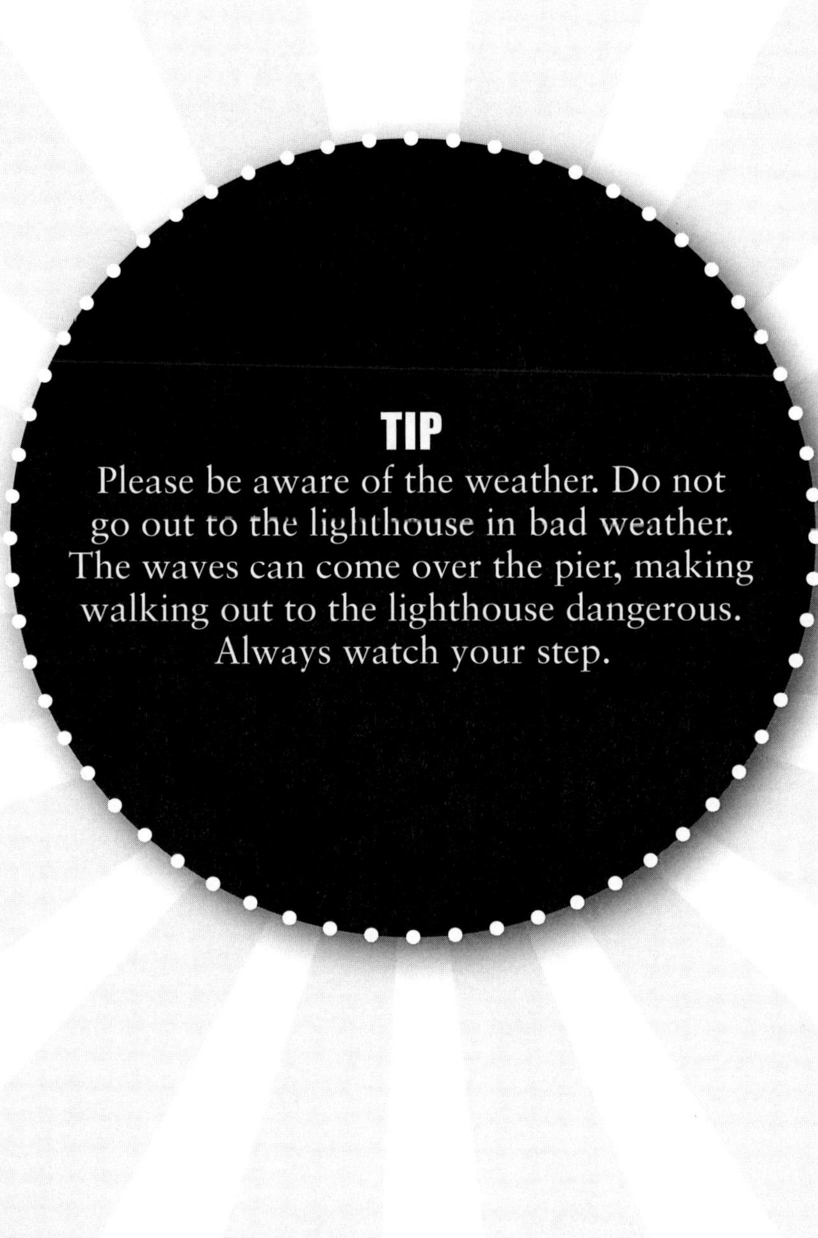

TIP

Please be aware of the weather. Do not go out to the lighthouse in bad weather. The waves can come over the pier, making walking out to the lighthouse dangerous. Always watch your step.

LOOK FOR PUBLIC ART
AROUND DOWNTOWN

Sheboygan's public art scene is growing every year. There are murals, sculptures, wrapped utility boxes, museums, and more that reflect Sheboygan's dedication to its public spaces. The Sheboygan Project in conjunction with the John Michael Kohler Arts Center and the Wooster Collective has created a mission to bring public art to the community. Many of this art is displayed on or around the high-traffic area around Eighth Street. There is also lots of art in unexpected places around Sheboygan. Don't forget to look up when you are near the Henry Jung Historic Apartments on S Eighth Street. You might spot *Billy Bud*, the cheerful chimney sweep sculpture that calls the top of the apartment building home.

You can get a walking-tour guide and map that spotlight the Sheboygan Project installations at the arts center or online.

Around Downtown
jmkac.org/engage-events/the-sheboygan-project

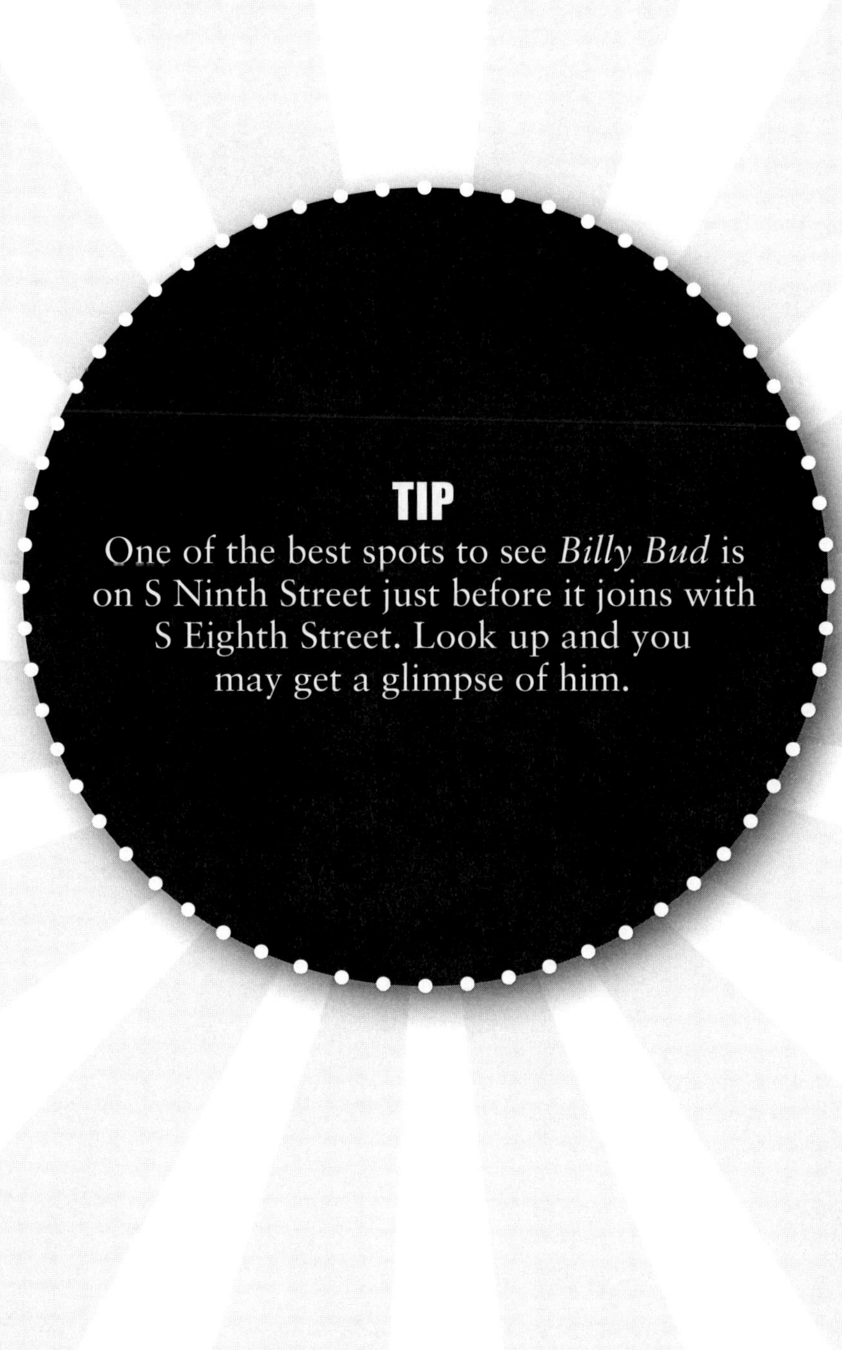

TIP

One of the best spots to see *Billy Bud* is on S Ninth Street just before it joins with S Eighth Street. Look up and you may get a glimpse of him.

LET THE KIDS EXPLORE
AT ABOVE & BEYOND CHILDREN'S MUSEUM

Fun and learning are on the menu at Above & Beyond Children's Museum. Kids interact with exhibits and immersive activities to learn about such things as gravity, making music on a PVC pipe organ, and different cultures to better understand our global community. Discover three floors and more than 10,000 square feet of fun, including a toddler area and a sky crawl that adults can use too.

Right outside to the north of the building is the new Purple Octopus Playground, an all-abilities play area that is ADA accessible. You cannot miss it. What I love is not only hearing the joy and laughter of the children when I walk by, but also how this colorful playground fits right into the downtown vibe.

After a visit to the museum, check out these nearby kid-friendly restaurants:

Above & Beyond Children's Museum
902 N 8th St., 920-458-4263
abkids.org

Driftwood
518 South Pier Dr., 920-287-7330
driftwoodsouthpier.com

Parker John's BBQ & Pizza
705 Riverfront Dr., 920-453-0299
parkerjohns.com

Black Pig
821 N 8th St., 920-457-6565
eatblackpig.com

Harry's Diner
2504 Calumet Dr., 920-458-5200

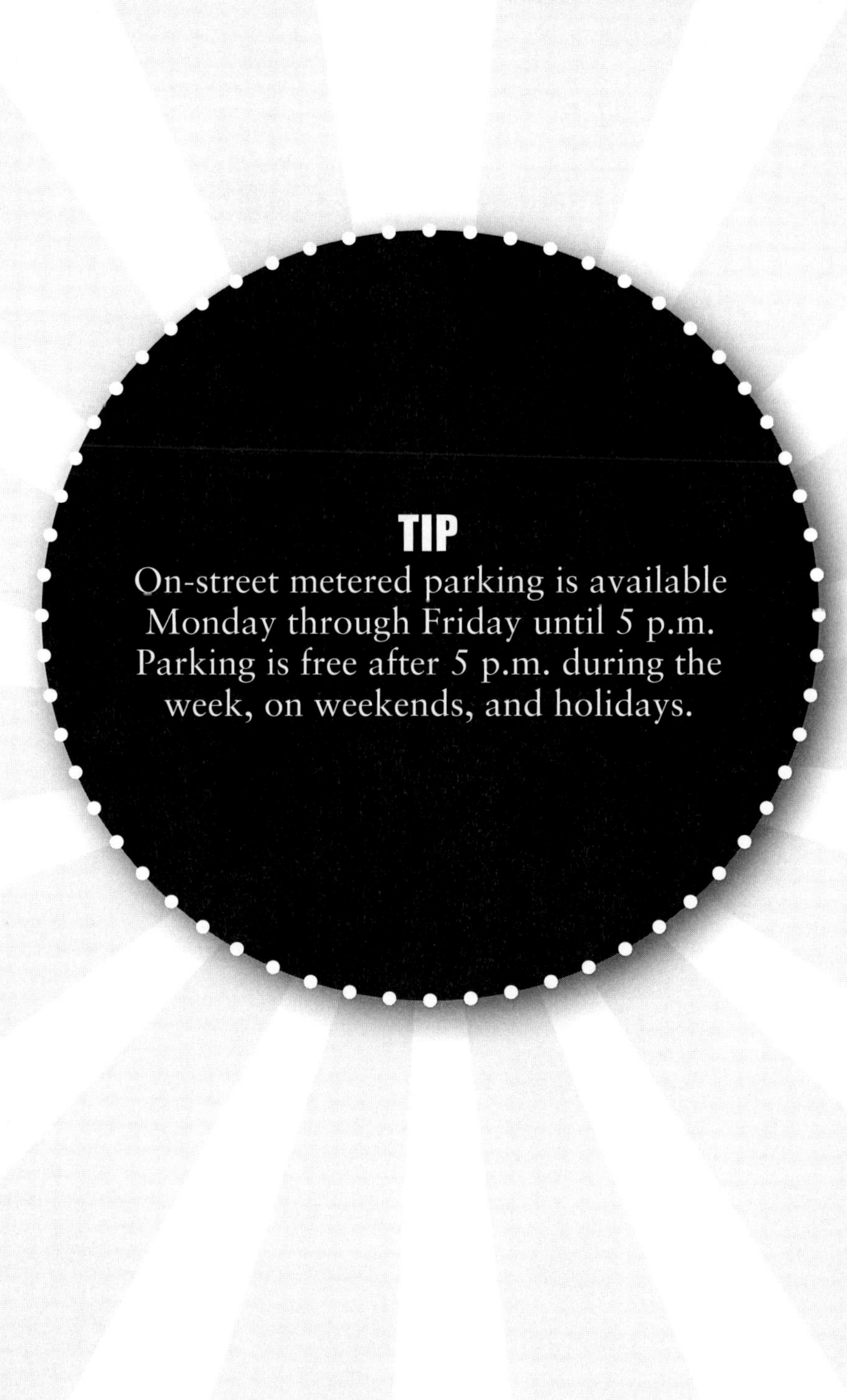
TIP
On-street metered parking is available Monday through Friday until 5 p.m. Parking is free after 5 p.m. during the week, on weekends, and holidays.

FIND OUT HOW
TECHNOLOGY AND FARMING INTERSECT AT FARM WISCONSIN DISCOVERY CENTER

Farm Wisconsin Discovery Center is a place of learning through interactive exhibits, a virtual tour of a real family farm, and observing the birth (if the timing is right) of a calf in the Birthing Barn. From finding out where your food comes from to learning how farmers are using advances in technology to improve their processes and use less land to produce more food, Farm Wisconsin offers a hands-on educational experience for all ages. First thing you can do when you enter and pay your admission is have the kiddos pretend they are milking a cow. Even if you have no interest in farming, I suggest you visit anyway. After all, we all eat, don't we?

You can easily spend a few hours here, and after you go through the exhibits, enjoy lunch in the café and an ice cream for dessert. You have to drive a few miles north out of Sheboygan to visit, but it's worth it.

7001 Gass Lake Rd., Manitowoc, 920-726-6000
farmwisconsin.org

TIP

There is a nice-sized gift shop inside the center. You can get all kinds of Wisconsin souvenirs and fun things for the kids.

SEE THE WORLD
AT VISIT SHEBOYGAN VISITOR CENTER

If you're visiting Sheboygan, the first place you'll want to stop is the Visit Sheboygan Visitor Center. Not only can you find out all the wonderful things you can do in Sheboygan and other parts of Wisconsin, but you can also grab some outstanding Sheboygan-themed merchandise. There's always something new: T-shirts, sweatshirts, pullovers, stickers, jewelry, and much more. You will find guidebooks from local authors, and you will maybe even find a copy of this book there.

The must-see at the visitor center is the *Science on a Sphere* exhibit. The screen is in the shape of a sphere and is really a giant animated planet. Visitors can access a multitude of online data from the National Oceanic and Atmospheric Administration (NOAA) including planes in flight across the world, wind and weather patterns, and population masses around the globe. All are displayed on the screen. If you drive by at night, the center glows with light from the sphere.

Certainly, this is one of the coolest visitor centers around.

826 S 8th St., 920-335-0060
visitsheboygan.com

SEE CHILDREN'S BOOKS COME ALIVE AT BOOKWORM GARDENS

Bookworm Gardens is a botanical garden that brings popular children's books to life, not to mention my favorite place in Sheboygan. From classics like *Goldilocks and the Three Bears* to modern titles like *Little Blue Truck*, Bookworm Gardens is a perfect place to explore no matter what your age.

The garden is divided into seven sections, each with a "book box" at the entrance with the books featured in the section. Reading the books adds to the experience of your visit. Inside each section is a collection of smaller gardens for each book.

Bookworm Gardens also has several other events during the season. The adult event, Boos and Brews, is held in early October. The garden takes on a spooky atmosphere with thousands of lights, live music, and food trucks. The whole family can come to Happily Haunted on several dates during the Halloween season, and the Secret Garden Summer Dinner Series sells out fast. Tickets are required for events, but you still can visit Bookworm Gardens anytime during the season.

1415 Campus Dr., 920-287-7895
bookwormgardens.org

The GameBoard

SHOPPING AND FASHION

PARTAKE IN THE THRILL OF THE HUNT

AT NIKKI'S NEX 2 NEW

The fashion hunt, that is. I adore thrifting and consignment shopping, and if you do too, step into Nikki's Nex 2 New and browse through the racks of carefully selected clothing, shoes, and accessories that are gently worn, or in some cases new. You can easily spend a few hours here. Nikki's accepts only the finest consignment pieces from popular chain stores like Banana Republic, lululemon, and J Crew and makes them affordable for everyone. The store is large, offering an extensive selection, and sorted by colors and sizes. There are also a couple of racks that feature favorite upscale brands such as Lilly Pulitzer, Free People, and Madewell. I even spotted a pair of Christian Louboutin white high-top sneakers that were in new condition on my last visit. They may have still been way out of my budget, but it was cool to see them.

There is a plus-size section as well as men's, children's, and infant sections. There is also a huge section with prom and formal dresses.

1019 N 8th St., 920-395-2442
nikkisnex2new.com

OTHER THRIFT, DISCOUNT, AND CONSIGNMENT SHOPS

City Vintage & Thrift

1131 N 8th St.

St. Vincent de Paul

4215 WI-42, 920-457-4844
svdpsheb.org

Sheboygan Discount Warehouse

2836 S Business Dr., 920-453-0363
sheboygandiscountwarehouse.com

Goodwill Store and Donation Center

3657 Greenwing Dr., 920-459-8600
amazinggoodwill.com

Richardson Hospice Resale Store

1130 Plankview Green Blvd., Sheboygan Falls
920-550-2114
ssrhospicehome.org/resale-store

UP YOUR GAME
AT THE GAMEBOARD

When some of us think of games, we think of the classics: Monopoly, Candy Land, and Old Maid. The GameBoard wants you to think of gaming as a way to educate, build cognitive learning, polish your social skills, and foster creativity. And I thought games were just supposed to be fun.

Stepping into the GameBoard is an experience.

Owner Lynn Poyton is a passionate advocate of games as a way to help all ages, those with disabilities, people recovering from brain injuries, and the elderly with dementia or in need of social time.

The shop is inside a historic building that was once a jewelry store. The dark-wood-and-glass display cases fit right in with the theme of the store. The shelves are filled with games, toys, and other merchandise. What is so unique is the knowledgeable staff who are all invested in the mission. You can rent games, and the store is a safe and welcoming place to socialize and play games with others.

621 N 8th St., 920-453-4263
the-gameboard.com

FIND YOUR NEXT FAVORITE BOOK
AT WORDHAVEN BOOKHOUSE

WordHaven BookHouse is everything a locally owned bookstore should be: welcoming, inclusive, and a safe place where you can be yourself. There are so many reasons why this is my favorite bookstore. Bright and colorful, with shelves upon shelves of new books, a downstairs area devoted to used books, and a comfy, quiet children's reading area. The walls are filled with art created by local artists. All the art is for sale.

Owner CJ is not only dedicated to supporting local authors but also other small businesses in the community. You will often find the bookstore hosting pop-up shops. There is an active events calendar, with in-store workshops, open mic nights, author signings, and a book club.

If you don't see the book you want in the store, or are not local, you can support WordHaven by going to the website and ordering books from there.

923 N 8th St., 920-395-2375
wordhaven-bookhouse.com

PERSONALIZE YOUR SKIN CARE
AT OLIVÜ 426

Affordable natural skin care made in-house. This is what you will find at Olivü 426. To think it all started with a homemade lip balm to help a friend who suffered injuries after a serious burning incident in 2003.

Owner Caitlin Brotz has built a local and national reputation for her skin care line. You will find products for your face—cleansers, serums, masks, and moisturizers—and body care items such as shampoo, body lotions, soaps, and scrubs. Olivü 426 uses quality ingredients and natural oils. You can purchase everything in the shop, and if you have questions about the products, the staff can answer them.

One of my favorite things is that you can personalize and add fragrances to certain products. So, you can pick out a bottle of shower soap or lotion and choose from the vast variety of scents at the scent bar to add. The only hard part is deciding which one. You can even create your own soap.

502 N 8th St., 920-783-0809
olivu426.com

RE-CREATE A LOST VINYL COLLECTION
AT THE MUSIC BOXX

Vinyl is alive and well, in case you didn't know. I am slowly trying to build my album collection after giving most of mine away years ago.

The place for vinyl in Sheboygan is Music Boxx Records. It's small inside, but the selection is excellent. Flipping through the cases and finding records that you thought were lost forever is an adrenaline rush. Along with a large selection of new and used records, they also have CDs, cassettes, and other music-related merchandise.

If you're in town for Record Store Day (RSD), stop in at the Music Boxx to (hopefully) snag a copy of a favorite new special release. Waiting in line before opening is a great way to strike up a music-related conversation with the people in line with you.

1119 N 8th St., 920-458-0951

LOOK FOR UNIQUE KITCHEN GADGETS
AT RELISH KITCHEN STORE

Are you a kitchen gadget geek? Do you need to have the latest baking tool? I'm not much of a cook, but I sure can spend hours looking at everything in a kitchen store, dreaming about what I could cook and bake.

This store is a treasure trove for anyone who enjoys spending time in the kitchen. From innovative tools you never knew you needed to high-quality, brand-name essentials from Zyliss and Zwilling that will elevate your culinary game, Relish has it all. This is also a great place to stop for the perfect wedding gift and gourmet food options.

The friendly staff is always ready to offer expert advice or demonstrate the latest gadgets, making your shopping experience both enjoyable and informative. Relish also has cooking and baking classes, and the website has a library of recipes.

811 N 8th St., 920-458-1898
relishkitchenstore.com

KEEP YOUR FEET WARM
WITH WIGWAM SOCKS

Wigwam began making socks here in Sheboygan in 1905. The company is now fourth-generation family-owned. Wigwam used to have an occasional sock sale selling factory seconds and overruns right at the factory. The popularity of the sale grew so much that now there is a dedicated outlet store called Wigwam Socks Outlet Store just outside Sheboygan.

Wigwam is known for producing high quality socks for runners, skiers, hunters, and hikers, and compression socks, all made right here in Sheboygan.

The outlet has a huge variety of socks and other knit merchandise for everyone in the family. The socks are comfy and come in fun colors, lengths, and sizes. The prices are fabulous. I always look for a pair of wool heavyweight socks that I wear in winter around the house. The store has limited hours.

5300 WI-42 N, 920-783-1080
wigwam.com

SHOP FOR TOYS
AT FREAKTOYZ

There once was a girl who loved collecting wrestling action figures. Her collection grew until years later when her mom started selling them. Fast-forward and now she is married and wants to replenish her collection. She and her husband started going to toy shows and flea markets. They ended up collecting way more than they needed, so they started selling some of them on the internet.

They soon turned their love of collecting and reselling vintage toys into a business, and the first Freaktoyz location was opened.

Melanie and Matthew Rieley now have a 4,000-square-foot space. They carry figures, comic books, video games, Funko Pop!s, and so much more. Stepping into the store is like a journey back in time for some, and for others it's a cool way to be introduced into toy history.

520 N 8th St., 920-287-7812
freaktoyz.com

REPLACE YOUR SOLE
AT MOLLY'S COBBLER SHOP

I adore this shop. The charm and curb appeal on the outside are enough to make you want to go inside. Molly's Cobbler Shop is a full-service shoe and leather repair shop. There are not many of these around anymore, so it's a delight that you can take a pair of shoes that you paid a lot of money for and give them new mileage with a repair. Owner Kevin also repairs Birkenstock shoe beds and soles.

The store has everything you need for your shoes and leather goods: shoelaces, leather lotion, and polishes.

In case you're just visiting and have no need for shoe or leather services, there is lots of unique Sheboygan merchandise to purchase: shirts, bags, postcards, and more. The merchandise Molly's carries makes fun gifts. This store is tiny, but it packs a mighty punch in personality.

1003 Michigan Ave., 920-452-7838
mollyscobblershop.com

TIP

Owner Kevin Hanson will also do custom leather projects.

INDULGE IN HOMEMADE CHOCOLATES
AT VICTORIAN CHOCOLATE SHOPPE

I don't know about you, but I have to visit every candy and ice cream shop at every destination I visit. Be prepared when you step in the door of the Victorian Chocolate Shoppe and the smell of sweetness and chocolate overtakes you. It's an absolute delight.

You are stepping inside another historic building in Sheboygan. This one is a former train and bus depot that has retained its original character on the outside.

Inside, you'll find a wide assortment of old-fashioned penny candy and hard-to-find confections. The spotlight, though, is on the chocolate. They are truffle experts. Can you believe there are truffles in 27 flavors? The shop also makes nut clusters, caramels, and turtles right there in the kitchen. I can never walk out of there without at least one truffle.

519 S 8th St., 920-453-0016
facebook.com/victorianchocolateshoppe

TIP

Try an Irish cream truffle and English toffee. Yum!

GET IN THE SPIRIT
WITH THE WINTER WONDERLAND AT CAAN'S FLORAL & GREENHOUSES

It's a tradition to visit Caan's Floral & Greenhouses at least once during the holiday season. There are Christmas trees decorated in all their finery, garland is draped everywhere, and the smell of pine lingers in the air. It's festive and colorful. If you can't get in the holiday spirit there, it might be a lost cause.

Go there to purchase winter centerpieces for inside and outside. You'll also find ornaments and holiday- and winter-themed wall hangings. You may even be able to make your own front door wreath during an on-site workshop.

November and December are not the only times to stop in. There's something blooming all year. In spring, the greenhouse bursts with color, and trees and shrubs line up outside, ready for planting. Flower arrangements are created during the wedding season, and fall is for pumpkins and mums.

4422 S 12th St., 920-452-4111
caanfloral.com

GET YOUR BUTTER
AT OLD WORLD CREAMERY

Wisconsin is the dairy state and we love our butter. Skip the grocery store and go right to the source to stock up. Old World Creamery has been making quality dairy products since 1912. It's still a family-owned company four generations later that continues the values from its beginnings.

Old World Creamery makes its delicious, creamy salted and unsalted butter on-site with milk from local dairy farms. The company also sells Irish butter. Old World Creamery imports European-style butter from Ireland; it's brought to Wisconsin where it goes through the grading process and then is packaged in the factory.

You can stop in the small store and purchase butter, cheese, and other dairy products as well as other Wisconsin food items. In my book, the butter is the reason for a visit. Don't forget to snap a selfie with the cow outside.

1606 Erie Ave., 920-593-9999
owcreamery.com

91

FIND BARGAIN ART SUPPLIES

AT HELLO HAPPINESS CREATIVITY CENTER

The themes are happiness, kindness, inspiration, and creativity, all rolled into one at Hello Happiness Creativity Center.

This is a place to let your imagination run wild. It's a retail space selling thrifted and new arts and crafts supplies. This helps make creativity accessible to everyone. The center accepts cash donations and donations of supplies. You can even visit the free corner.

Hello Happiness has a studio where classes, events, and demonstrations take place. It's filled with materials and is a welcoming, fun, and innovative place where adults and teens come to play through creation, from scrapbooking to jewelry making.

The center is a nonprofit started by Kim Geiser. She has had many creative endeavors in the past. The idea came to her to create a place where everyone could come and create as well as have access to affordable supplies, so no one is excluded. The community has gotten behind the Hello Happiness Creativity Center.

1504 New Jersey Ave., 920-783-6152
hellohappinesscreativitycenter.com

92

LOAD UP
ON JOHNSONVILLE BRATS AT JOHNSONVILLE MARKETPLACE

Most people across the country recognize the popular Johnsonville brand for its delicious sausages, brats, and other meat products. When the Johnsonville Marketplace opened in late 2020, it quickly became a must-visit destination for both locals and visitors, offering all things Johnsonville in one convenient location. The 3,200-square-foot store not only carries the iconic food products that made Johnsonville famous, such as brats, summer sausage, and breakfast links, but also a variety of branded merchandise. You can find fun items like Johnsonville clothing (yes, even brat-themed socks), tailgating gear like grilling accessories and games, and unique gifts for the sausage lover in your life.

One of the highlights of visiting the marketplace is the chance to discover rare and limited-edition products, including Irish O' Garlic Sausages and Johnsonville Foodservice items. It's a treasure trove for anyone wanting to explore nearly every product the company has ever made.

N6877 Rio Rd., 920-453-5678
johnsonvillemarketplace.com

TIP

You can always order online and you can return products within 30 days.

SUPPLY YOUR ARTISTIC SIDE
AT AMPERSAND SUPPLY CO.

Unleash your creativity and fuel your artistic passions at Ampersand Supply Co. This vibrant store is a haven for artists, crafters, and anyone with a creative spark.

Whether you're a professional artist or a hobbyist looking to explore new mediums, Ampersand Supply Co. has everything you need to bring your ideas to life. I can spend a couple hours here. From high-quality paints and brushes to unique papers and crafting materials, every corner of the store is filled with inspiration. The knowledgeable staff is always eager to help you find the perfect tools and supplies, making it easy to dive into your next project with confidence.

You can also sign up for one of the many classes or workshops to fuel your creative side with fellow artists.

1212 N 8th St., 920-287-3268
ampersandsupplyco.com

94

BROWSE THE LATEST IN FASHION AT KNOT & THREAD

Sheboygan has some fantastic boutiques for women, and this is one of them. The nice thing is that most of these are all in the downtown area, so you can park your car once and make an afternoon of it.

Knot & Thread is a one-stop shop for stylish women's clothing, socks, inspirational items, and home decor. I love the fresh styles here (and fun graphic tees), and they also have cool Sheboygan gear. The handmade wooden bowls are unique, functional art pieces and make great gifts. Everything is arranged nicely, and the atmosphere is warm and friendly. Some clothing items are available in sizes up to 3X. Grab your friends and go on a little downtown Sheboygan shopping spree. Retail therapy is good for the soul.

514 N 8th St.
facebook.com/knotnthread

MORE CLOTHING BOUTIQUES IN SHEBOYGAN

Anna's Unique Boutique

818 Erie Ave., 920-980-7269

Mainstream Boutique

723 N 8th St., 920-395-2148
mainstreamboutiquesheboygan.com

TLC Casuals

635 Riverfront Dr., 920-451-3084
tlccasuals.com

GET ON YOUR BIKE AND RIDE AT SULLY'S RIDE SHOP

Sully's Ride Shop isn't just about motorcycles; it's about embracing and promoting a full biker lifestyle. Stepping into this stylish shop feels like entering a cool community hub where riders gather to swap stories, share maintenance tips, and celebrate their passion for the open road. The biker merchandise at Sully's goes beyond the typical, offering chic, upscale items that blend fashion and function. The team takes pride in curating products that meet three essential principles: safety, style, and durability.

Even though I'm not a motorcycle rider myself, I wouldn't hesitate to stop by. Not only does Sully's offer an excellent selection of gifts for motorcycle enthusiasts, but I'm sure I'd find something that catches my eye as well. Whether you ride or not, the shop's unique vibe and high-quality items make it a fun and interesting place to explore.

815 N 8th St., 920-395-2572
sullysrideshop.com

TAKE GUITAR LESSONS
AT LAKESIDE MUSIC

Lakeside Music is your go-to store for all things music, and it's proudly family owned. With two locations—one in Port Washington and another right here in Sheboygan—it's a full-service music haven. Whether you're looking for guitar lessons, musical instruments (both new and used), sheet music, or rentals, Lakeside Music has you covered. As a ukulele fan myself, I was thrilled to discover that they offer ukulele lessons too! The store itself is clean, straightforward, and designed with musicians in mind.

If you've got an instrument in need of repair, Lakeside's got that covered as well. They even provide appraisals if you're curious about the value of your instrument. And if you're shopping for something new, the knowledgeable staff is always ready to help you find the perfect instrument to suit your needs. Whether you're a beginner or a seasoned player, Lakeside Music is a must-visit.

809 S 8th St., 920-452-8641
lakesidemusicstore.com

PICK UP SOME FABULOUS WINE
AT SOLU ESTATE WINERY

It was hard to figure out what category to put SoLu Estate under. For one thing, the property is huge. It's situated in the Kettle Moraine, so the setting is gorgeous. Weekly events are going on all summer. They have music on two stages with abundant seating.

Of course, it's a winery first. The winery grows 14 different varieties of grapes, and it also operates its own meadery.

If you are not familiar with mead, it is really in a class by itself. Mead is made with honey as its sugar source. Yeast and water are added, then it's fermented to the proper alcohol level and either served like that or flavored with fruit, herbs, or spices.

For me, this is the place to go to just walk in the store, maybe sit at the bar for a tasting to decide which ones I like and purchase them. There are snacks for sale in the store to enjoy with your wine or mead.

W8269 County Rd. F, Cascade, 920-528-1550
soluestate.com

PICK OUT A FANTASTIC BABY GIFT AT BLUEBIRD BABY & KIDS BOUTIQUE

I've found the essential shop for a fabulous baby shower gift. Don't you feel warm and fuzzy when you walk into a baby shop? I know I do. There's just something about the tiny onesies, colorful board books, and stuffed toys that can melt anyone's heart.

Stepping inside the woman-owned Bluebird Baby & Kids Boutique gives that feeling in aces. This is the one-stop shop in Sheboygan for all baby and toddler needs. This shop has everything for baby up to the toddler stage: learning toys, accessories, the cutest clothing, board books, and much more. There is a baby registry for new parents, and the store has warm personalized service. You do not need to shop anywhere else. Bluebird is the best place to find the perfect baby gift. The shop is located across from Blue Harbor Resort.

534 South Pier Dr., 920-395-3751
bluebirdsheboygan.com

99

FIND YOUR BAIT

AT JEFF'S TACKLE / THE WHARF

Are you heading out on the lake? You'll find all your fishing needs at the Wharf. This cute little weathered shack on the riverfront may not look like your typical bait shop, but it certainly has all the supplies you need for a day on the water. That includes drinks and snacks. Plus, the Wharf offers rod and reel repair and fish cleaning, cutting, and smoking. The Wharf also holds fishing derbies like the Powder Puff Derby and the junior derby throughout the season. The whole family can participate.

Also, you can always stop in for a rest from walking the boardwalk and have an ice cream on a hot summer day. Who knows, you might even get to hear some mighty fish tales from the locals.

733 Riverfront Dr., 920-458-4406
facebook.com/JeffsTackle

BROWSE HANDCRAFTED ITEMS
AT 3ELEPHANTS & COMPANY

I usually make it a point to stop in craft and artisan shops when I travel. You might stumble upon a local artisan who comes up with a creative idea, something you've never seen before, and you just have to have it. These are the places to find unique gifts from local crafters. That's just what 3Elephants & Company is.

The shop offers vendors a place to sell their wares in one spot. Each vendor has their own space set up the way they want. The vendors change their merchandise often. You can find lots of seasonal items, plus jewelry, home decor, crocheted hats and scarves, and coffee mugs in a fun and attractive space. It's great to support microbusinesses like these who need a place to sell their wares.

1503 N 8th St., 920-917-3377

Kohler-Andrae State Park

ACTIVITIES
BY SEASON

WINTER

Get in the Spirit with the Winter Wonderland at Caan's Floral & Greenhouses, 121

Practice Your Swing at Golf 365, 81

Learn About Artist-Built Environments at John Michael Kohler Art Preserve, 90

Experience Winter Fun at Blue Harbor Resort, 64

SPRING

See the Model Railroads at Sheboygan Railroad Museum, 88

Try Your Hand at Axe Throwing at Longhouse Axe Bar, 63

Climb Parnell Tower, 62

Learn Why Sheboygan Was Once Known as "Chair City" at the Sheboygan County Museum, 92

SUMMER

FALL

SUGGESTED
ITINERARIES

OUTDOOR ESCAPES

Hook a Catch of the Day on a Fishing Charter, 52

Watch the Sunrise from South Pier, 77

Spend a Day at Road America, 51

Hike or Snowshoe the Ice Age Trail, 70

Hit the Trail at Kohler-Andrae State Park, 56

Swim at Deland Park and North Beach, 66

FUN FOR THE KIDS

Hit the Mini Links at Harbor Pointe Mini Golf, 78

Find Out How Technology and Farming Intersect at Farm Wisconsin Discovery Center, 104

See the Model Railroads at Sheboygan Railroad Museum, 88

Let the Kids Explore at Above & Beyond Children's Museum, 102

Experience Winter Fun at Blue Harbor Resort, 64

Get an Ice Cream at South Pier Parlor, 25

See Children's Books Come Alive at Bookworm Gardens, 107

UNIQUELY SHEBOYGAN

Have a Brat Plate at Sly's Midtown Salooon, 18

Take a Surfing Lesson with EOS Surf Shop, 50

• •

FOR THE FOODIES

HISTORY BUFFS

INDEX

CITY
Sheboygan's
Hearth Baked Rolls &
Authentic Fleishbrok & Bavarian
Presenting
Artisan
All Occasion
Fresh Quality
City Bakery